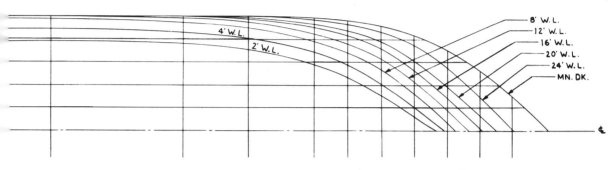

HALF-BREADTH PLAN

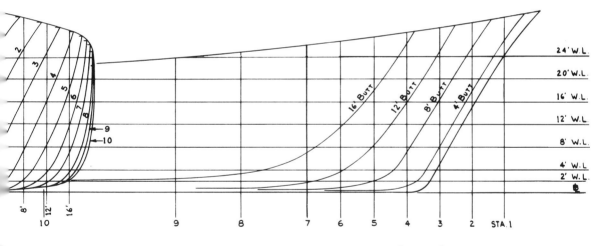

SHEER PLAN

Four-Masted Schooner, *Purnell T. White*
Drawn by Robert F. Sumrall
Courtesy: The Mariners Museum

Sea, Sails and Shipwreck

Career of the four-masted schooner, *Purnell T. White*

Purnell T. White, as painted by the marine artist Antonio Jacobsen, 1919. Author's Collection

Sea, Sails and Shipwreck

Career of the four-masted schooner
Purnell T. White

By ROBERT H. BURGESS

TIDEWATER PUBLISHERS

1970   Cambridge, Maryland

ISBN 0-87033-147-7

Library of Congress Catalog Card Number: 73-124313

Printed in the United States of America

Copyright © 1970 by Tidewater Publishers

All Rights Reserved

Dedication

To my wife

ADELE

who prowled the hulk of the *Purnell T. White* with me in 1936 and has heard that name mentioned in our household these many years as if the old schooner were a member of the family.

Other Books by Robert H. Burgess

THIS WAS CHESAPEAKE BAY

CHESAPEAKE CIRCLE

COASTING CAPTAIN (Edited)

STEAMBOATS OUT OF BALTIMORE (Collaborated)

Contents

Acknowledgments

AS THE pieces of a jigsaw puzzle eventually fit together, so it is with maritime research. I had considerable material on the schooner *Purnell T. White* in my personal collection after about 40 years of assiciation with that ship. But I gave no thought of ever compiling it into book form. When I did decide to try to assemble a fairly round image of that vessel and her activities I realized there were things I still needed. But where to find them at this late date? I had never seen a view of the schooner in frame on the building ways; a portrait of her builder would be appropriate. Did pictures of the vessel's namesake, or the young lady who christened her, exist? Could any of her logbooks be found? Was it possible to trace her career, voyage by voyage? Who held ownership in the schooner?

I knew that A. James Conley, a son of her builder, lived at Fruitland, near Salisbury, Maryland. A visit to his home netted a picture of his father. Another son, John R. Conley, of Seaford, Delaware, sent me views of the *White* under construction and a striking scene of her when she left the builder's yard. At the conclusion of a lecture I delivered in Snow Hill, Maryland, in late 1969, I voiced a plea for material on the old schooner. Mrs. William P. Phillips, of Berlin, Maryland, stepped forward and advised me that her mother had christened the *Purnell T. White* and she was the niece of the man for whom the schooner was named. She supplied me with photographs of both individuals.

An important source was Charles C. Paul, grandson of the Baltimore shipbroker C. C. Paul whose firm owned many schooners and shares in the *White*. Mr. Charles C. Paul had saved notebooks and ledgers from his family's business and permitted me to make copies of these for inclusion in this book.

As the result of an article I had written about the *Purnell T. White* in the August 1953 issue of the magazine *Ships and the Sea,* I received a letter from James S. McCullough who had sailed in the schooner in 1933. Correspondence ensued over the years and revealed that he had taken a number of photographs during that voyage. He eventually wrote several articles about his trip which were published in the *Nautical Research Journal* in 1959-60. This was the best account I had ever read of life aboard, and the handling of, a four-masted coasting schooner. It is included in its entirety in this volume through the courtesy of the *Journal* and Mrs. James S. McCullough. A selection of Mr. McCullough's photographs taken on board the *White* at sea illustrate his account.

Thanks to H. I. Chapelle, Smithsonian Institution, for arranging to have the lines taken off the half model of the *Purnell T. White* at the Maryland Historical Society, and to Robert F. Sumrall for drawing up these lines to serve as the endpapers of this volume.

I was not present when the *White* was released from her first site of abandonment in 1957 but Mr. John F. Golden, an engineer on that project, was on the spot and through him I received photographs of the clearing away of debris and her eventual flotation.

Others who have supplied photographs or assistance were Francis E. Bowker, Miss Myrtle M. Gantt, William L. Earll, Joseph C. B. White, F. Verbeeck, William H. Swan, John A. Noble, U. S. Coast Guard, E. P. Griffith–The Mariners Museum, *Nautical Research Journal,* Norfolk News-papers, *Baltimore Sun, Baltimore News,* National Archives, *Nautical Gazette,* A. Aubrey Bodine, and the Maryland Historical Society. I also wish to thank William T. Radcliffe, photographer at The Mariners Museum, New-port News, Virginia, for his expert copying of some of the old and faded photographs and documents.

The excellent book *Coast Guard to the Rescue,* by Karl Baarslag, con-tained a dramatic account of the loss of the *Purnell T. White,* the only acknowledgment to that fine schooner I have ever seen in a book except in my own writings. It was good to have this last phase of her active career recorded in that volume which served as a reference.

The jigsaw puzzle probably could be more complete. Several pieces are still missing and may be lost forever in the shuffle of time. I would have liked to have had additional first-hand accounts of passages in this schooner. However, it is most likely that all who crewed in her have passed on. I am one of the few still around who even trod her deck. Perhaps the publication of this book will bring forth some material of interest and value. It usually works out that way. Even though it would be too late for inclusion, it will be good to know of its existence to further document the career of one of the more successful and colorful coasting schooners.

Introduction

THE four-masted schooner *Purnell T. White* was certainly not the most photographed sailing ship. However, it is rather safe to say that few, if any, vessels have been photographed so completely "from the cradle to the grave." Building and launching scenes of various ships are numerous. These might be followed by a portrait of the vessel under sail, at anchor, in tow, or at a pier done by a commercial photographer who had been hired by the vessel's owner or captain. Then sometime in the ship's career she might have come within a camera's range if some disaster overtook her, if she set a record of sorts, or if some ship fancier made an effort to preserve his own record of the vessel.

Prior to the 1930's the seaman rarely included a camera in his seabag or suitcase as he embarked on a voyage. What he expected to encounter was just another trip usually made up of hard work, long hours and, quite often, poor food. Why photograph anything responsible for that? To be sure, the passing years mellowed his memories and he would discuss his travels and probably wished he had pictures to show to assist his tale. But at the moment of the actual event, the act of recording it on film was usually farthest from his thoughts. Considering the countless voyages made by ships of all kinds, relatively few scenes of shipboard activities exist. And once that vessel was cast aside or abandoned, she was dismissed from the minds of most.

To narrow this down to the type of ship represented in this volume, a schooner that ranged along the American east coast and occasionally down to South America, West Indies, the Gulf, and on transatlantic voyages, their deckhands were not conscious of preserving an historical or documentary record of the ship. Theirs was just a job for which they were meagerly paid. If the thought had occurred to them they probably felt they could not have afforded the cost of a camera and film, or they lacked the knowledge to operate it. Yet many of the existing shipboard scenes and other maritime views were made with simple equipment like fixed-focus cameras requiring virtually no adjustments. All one had to do was load the camera with film, be sure of sufficient light, try to hold the camera steady, and click the shutter. But even this was beyond the interest or comprehension of most seamen. They lacked awareness or, to put it more bluntly, they were "too close to the forest to see the trees."

It was when sailing ships had virtually disappeared that the camera was put to full use in recording their activities. The bulk of views taken on board coasting schooners at sea probably occurred during the 1930's. An occasional snapshot would have been taken at any time when cameras were in relatively common use but this was usually of crew members posing individually or in a group and not when they were about their business of sailing the ship or depicting general deck views of the vessel at sea.

On rare occasions the captain or mates may have had a camera. Some of the most dramatic views of the five-masted schooner *Edna Hoyt* in heavy weather were taken with a box camera by Captain George H. Hopkins during that vessel's last voyage in 1937. If a seaman were younger and of the late period, he may have had a camera with his personal gear; but the older hands made no attempt to preserve any of their workaday world. Theirs was a dollar a day and keep and that was usually the extent of interest in their surroundings.

In 1936 I sailed on the four-masted schooner *Doris Hamlin* out of Baltimore on a three-month voyage to Newport News, Bermuda, Haiti, and return. I was aware that I was participating in a disappearing trade and boarded the vessel with a good camera and many rolls of film. By the end of the voyage I had taken about 200 photographs of the schooner, its crew, shipboard scenes, and loading methods. Virtually every view is a priceless documentary of a type of ship that no longer exists. One could rarely take a photograph of or on board one of these big schooners that did not result in a view of artistic or documentary value. Had I not taken these pictures, I would still have my journal of the trip to recall the events but that would be a poor second to the actual photographs.

The same holds true with the views of the *Purnell T. White* included in the illustrations in this volume. My visits on board the vessel when she was active and later as a hulk are still recalled with pleasure. But when those memories are revived and the photographs are there to supplement the mental image, they are ever so much more meaningful.

By searching far and wide, and utilizing my own photographs, I have assembled a rather complete photographic history of the career of the schooner *Purnell T. White*. I was fortunate to have been a native of Baltimore where this vessel and others like her called. I was attracted to them and directed my camera at them. But now they have all disappeared. The *White,* as illustrated in this book and preserved for all time, is the sole example to depict the full and somewhat rigorous life of a Chesapeake-built coasting schooner. It is a deserving tribute for she was a handsome ship and did her job well.

ROBERT H. BURGESS

Chapter 1

THE big schooner's graceful sheer was accentuated by the straight, stark lines of the Pratt Street, Baltimore, pier at which she lay. From the tip of her tapering, needlelike jibboom, pointing at a skyward angle, the sweep of her lines trailed aft to a gentle, rising curve culminating at her shapely stern. Not exactly big for a vessel of her rig, she did, however, overshadow the somewhat jaunty and delicate looking Chesapeake Bay two-masted schooners moored nearby.

This impressive schooner was the four-masted *Purnell T. White,* one of the last vessels thus rigged to be built in the Chesapeake Bay area and one of the few still plying the American east coast in the early 1930's. Just in from the sea and almost yachtlike in appearance, except for the workaday look of her salt-streaked sides and stains from her freeing ports, she was snugged down with her sails neatly stowed and her burdensome deck cargo of lumber secured by upright stakes and chains. Another load had been delivered safely after a brief confrontation with a winter storm as she made her way up the coast to Chesapeake Bay from Georgetown, South Carolina.

A few days earlier the maritime columns of the Baltimore newspapers had expressed concern as she went unreported for several days after a gale had lashed the coast. It seemed that if she failed to adhere to a schedule the newsmen set up for her—so many days from port to port—she was always a good subject for a "posted missing" story. And on this occasion they had played up that angle to the hilt.

These news releases about the *White* had kept her to the fore and whenever I knew she was in port I would make my way to the waterfront to stand and admire, what was in my eyes, this magnificent ship. A mere lad in knee breeches, I was attracted to the docks by the romance attached to this schooner and there began a "love affair" that exists today even though the vessel has long departed from the sea-lanes. From the days when she was stout and strong, to the end when her timbers could crumble between my fingers, I visited the *Purnell T. White* as an old friend whenever possible. Those latter years were sad ones, as when one recalls a youth in his prime and then witnesses his decline to infirmity.

When I was a youngster, I spoke of the *White* on as intimate terms as many of my boyhood chums discussed Jimmy Foxx, Babe Ruth, and Lou Gehrig. As they followed the careers of their athletic heroes and were able to recite their standings and records, I knew all the statistics of this schooner, such as when and where built, dimensions, tonnage, and trades.

The graceful sheer of the *Purnell T. White* is evident in this view at the James Lumber Company, Baltimore, on February 25, 1931. Photo: Author

The author, as a boy, at the steering wheel of the *White* at James Lumber
Company, Baltimore, February 25, 1931. Photo: Author

A lumber cargo from Georgetown, South Carolina, is discharged from the *Purnell T. White* at Baltimore, February 25, 1931. Photo: Author

When they checked the papers for the positions of the ball clubs, my eyes were on the shipping columns for news of the *Purnell T. White* and others like her.

4

Looking aft on the deck of the *White* at Baltimore, February 25, 1931.
Photo: Author

The author stands beside the port quarterboard of the *Purnell T. White*, February 25, 1969. Photo: William T. Radcliffe

It was somewhat disappointing to see this schooner, that I had associated with the clean, deep waters of the sea, in the turbid backwaters of Baltimore harbor. I could envision her under full sail rising on the crest of a large sea and then plunging downward as it rolled on and another followed behind to lift her stern. It seemed that these visits to port were merely something for her to endure, to discharge her cargo, and be on her way again. As the lumber was taken out of her hold she lightened and each day a new oil-stained waterline marked her sides. Soot from nearby factories sifted down on her cabins and decks and she seemed contaminated from the city's grime. If a charter were not available when she was ready for sea again, weeks of exposure to this degrading atmosphere ensued. But that charter did come and her sails were bent and her decks and cabins scrubbed down as she prepared to take a tow down the Chesapeake to her sea route again. When many large schooners were idling in port for lack of cargoes during those depression years, the *White* kept busy. Most of those vessels waited in vain for freights that never came, were neglected, and eventually abandoned.

In port, except for the stevedores removing her lumber, she almost seemed deserted. But, invariably, the cook remained on board and he could be seen shuffling about the deck or splitting wood for his cookstove. One could board her without any objection. Actually, few paid heed to the big sailing ships in those days so there was no fear of visits from the throngs. The surroundings of the piers were just not conducive to visits from the average sightseer. And who cared about such a misfit, anyway; one shunted to less attractive waterfront areas and completely out of keeping with the trend toward progress? Ah, thirty years hence they would gladly pay a price to gaze at her or trod her decks! But earlier I had her to myself and alone appreciated her breed.

What ship-struck youngster hasn't been fascinated by a large sailing vessel? And if he had read sea stories woven around these ships, and was fortunate enough to have known them firsthand, as I did the *White* and others of her rig which called at Baltimore, these tales would suddenly come to life. Here was a living marine museum! These big coasting schooners were virtually obsolete and one of the last links with the great days of sail. Canvas, hemp, huge wooden blocks, belaying pins, windlass, capstan—all in use and doing a necessary task at that time. Now one has to visit a landbound museum to view most of these items. A stroll on the quarterdeck would bring to mind some of the conversations which might have taken place in times of storm or placid trade-wind sailing. Just what ports had this schooner visited since she left the building ways? What would the future hold for her? Some of these answers I knew even as I walked her decks as a boy. Others I was to learn as her career progressed and we both grew older in our separate ways. There was no way then for me to see the violent end in store for her. Nor could I even imagine the state of neglect and total deterioration that was to befall her. Through the three decades and more that followed those days when I visited her as a lad, I was to witness a ship endure treatment as no other vessel I have ever known. And she withstood it as long as her timbers held together—all credit to her Maryland builders.

Carved, wooden figurehead from the *Purnell T. White*. Author's Collection.

In all the years I have known the *Purnell T. White* I have never been very far removed from her. I photographed her religiously over a period of 40 years. I have had various relics from her in my home and office. After she arrived in Baltimore following her dismasting in 1934, I secured a belaying pin, jib hank, and portions of her foremast and spanker. Several years later I was given the sextant belonging to her last master who was lost from the vessel, Captain Charles Nicklas. This instrument was found in the wreckage of his cabin and turned over to R. B. White, managing owner of the schooner. He eventually gave it to Captain George H. Hopkins, then master of the Baltimore four-masted schooner *Doris Hamlin*. I sailed in the latter vessel with Captain Hopkins and, knowing of my interest in the *White*, he passed the sextant along to me.

After the *Purnell T. White* was abandoned in a Baltimore ships' graveyard, I salvaged her port quarterboard, where her name was carved, and it now hangs above my desk. From my earliest association with this schooner I admired the carving of an eagle's head staring ahead from the top of her cutwater. That figurehead was with the *White* during her entire active career and shared with her the numerous landfalls and departures, lifted with her bows in Atlantic and Caribbean seas, knew the tropics and winter gales, and survived them all.

While vandals picked her bones to salvage scrap metal for monetary gain, I was intent on recovering her figurehead to help keep her memory alive. Off and on for 18 years, after she arrived in port for the last time in 1934, I made attempts to free this bird from its lofty and almost inaccessible perch. It was in an awkward position and there was no rigging to cling to or to act as leverage in a prying operation. The girth of the bowsprit also thwarted several tries. A bos'n's chair was secured and I suspended myself beneath the carving but it still refused to come loose with a crowbar or saw. I did manage to salvage a portion of it and I saved this with the hope that someday I would obtain the entire carving and be able to reassemble it.

In 1952 I was visiting the Vane Brothers' ship chandlery on Pratt Street, Baltimore, and was discussing my many attempts to retrieve the *White's* figurehead. Present was Captain Norman E. Horstman, skipper of Vane's harbor chandlery boat, who informed me that he had salvaged the carving. He was passing by the schooner's hulk earlier after making a delivery and saw the weathered eagle still in position. He eased his boat under the hulk's longhead, threw a line over the carving, and forged ahead slowly, pulling the line taut. The soft pine pins which held the carving in a slot gave way under the pressure and the eagle's head fell in the boat's wake. Horstman recovered the figurehead, placed it in the engine room, and didn't give too much thought to it thereafter. As I spoke to him he told me that his boat was to be inspected and he had no place to put this "bird." He sensed my sincere interest in the carving and gave it to me. Like fitting a lost piece into a jigsaw puzzle, the broken portion of the carving that I had salvaged years before was fastened to the figurehead and it was made whole. Today it gazes from a perch in my den with a rather wistful look in its eyes as though it were reminiscing about the many voyages it had made as a part of the *Purnell T. White*.

9

In the process of gathering data for this volume I contacted heirs of C. C. Paul and Company, Baltimore ship brokers who owned shares in the *Purnell T. White*. My correspondent was Charles C. Paul, grandson of the founder of the firm who willingly loaned me material that had been saved from the brokerage office. On one occasion he visited me and brought additional news clippings and photographs he had found. Then he handed me a package, flat and rectangular in shape, and said, "This is for you." I carefully removed the paper wrapping and there was a portrait of the *Purnell T. White* painted in oil by the marine artist Antonio Jacobsen in 1919. Jacobsen had done a number of these and I had seen others of the *White*, or knew of their existence, in Baltimore, Norfolk, Delaware, and on the Eastern Shore of Maryland. Now I had one to round out my collection of material dealing with the venerable schooner. A slight mist came to my eyes as I looked at the colorful portrait, a broadside view showing her in full sail, recalling the days when I knew her as depicted in the painting and comparing that with her appearance today. But the fact that I had known her at all was a great privilege and the portrait will ever keep her alive.

Chapter 2

THE *Purnell T. White* was a product of the World War I shipbuilding boom. As the merchant steamships were sunk in great numbers by German U-boats, in addition to building steel and wooden steamers to replace them, American shipyards constructed scores of four-masted schooners in East, West, and Gulf coast ports. Maine was the chief producer of this type of vessel. Only four were built in the Chesapeake Bay area from 1917 to 1919, three of these in Maryland and one at Seaford, Delaware, on the Nanticoke River, a tributary flowing into the bay. The *White* was one of these, built in 1917, at Sharptown, Maryland. For the record, the others were the *Charles M. Struven* in 1917, at Pocomoke City, Maryland; *Alexander H. Erickson* in 1918, at Seaford, Delaware; the *Anandale* in 1919, at Sharptown. The *Purnell T. White* was to outlast these at sea under sail. The *Struven* carried on the longest. After she was converted to a barge in 1929, and renamed the *Maurice R. Shaw, Jr.,* she was towed along the coast until foundering on November 4, 1942, off Point Jupiter Light, Florida.

Sharptown is situated on the east side of the Nanticoke River, 28 miles above the mouth. This had been a shipbuilding town for many years and the following entry appears in the *U. S. Coast Pilot* for the year the *White* was built: ". . . There is a shipyard, and a marine railway capable of hauling out vessels of 1,000 tons, 200 feet length, 7 feet draft forward and 13 feet aft." This was one of the largest shipyards on the Eastern Shore of Maryland and was known as the Sharptown Marine Railway.

R. B. White, a partner in the firm of C. C. Paul and Company, ship brokers of Baltimore, was one of the principals behind the construction of the *White.* In May 1916, the three-masted schooner *R. B. White,* owned by C. C. Paul and Company, was sold for about $33,000 to the Franklin Baker Cocoanut Company. Perhaps Mr. White desired a larger schooner to take advantage of the many freights available at the time. Tragically, the *R. B. White,* sailing from Philadelphia on September 7, 1916, with 8 on board, was posted missing and not since heard from.

Apparently, R. B. White lost little time in contracting for a new schooner. Shipyards along the Maine coast were busy constructing the big coasting schooners. The 147-foot *R. B. White* had been built at Millbridge, Maine, in 1912, so owner White may have preferred down-east vessels. But he no doubt wanted a schooner as quickly as possible and decided upon the Sharptown Marine Railway. This was a wise choice as that shipyard was relatively close to Baltimore and the builders and owner could keep in close touch. Too, that upper Nanticoke River region was noted for its sturdy ships and the shipbuilding skills of many of its residents; less than 10 miles from Sharptown was Bethel, Delaware, situated on Broad Creek, making off the Nanticoke, where wooden sailing vessels had been built for years. These towns were surrounded by forests bearing ideal shipbuilding timbers.

Half model of the *Purnell T. White* in the collection of the Maryland Historical Society, Baltimore, Maryland. Photo: Author

The four-masted schooner *Purnell T. White* takes shape on the building ways of the Sharptown Marine Railway, Sharptown, Maryland. Looking aft in the framed hull, with her designer and builder Alonzo R. Conley at left. Photo: John R. Conley

By early February 1917, the new schooner was well under way and her fittings were being discussed via letters between R. B. White and his brother Purnell and Alonzo Conley, misspelled Connolly in the letter.* Conley is credited with having been the designer and builder of the *White*. The Milford vessel referred to in the letter was the four-masted schooner *Albert F. Paul* being constructed at Milford, Delaware for C. C. Paul and Company and launched in August 1917.

---

* *See* Appendix.

In April 1917, the *Nautical Gazette* reported that the Sharptown Marine Railway was hurrying to complete a four-masted schooner for R. B. White. ". . . It is expected to have her in the water within six weeks." Some delays were encountered, however, and it was midsummer before the hull was waterborne.

On August 22, 1917, the launching party had gathered at the Sharptown shipyard. This was a big event in that little town. It had been 10 years since the last four-masted schooner slid into the Nanticoke River from a Sharptown shipyard. That vessel was the *Albert W. Robinson*. In 1910, the four-masted schooner *Anna R. Heidritter* had been launched there but she had been rebuilt from the remains of the *Cohasset* which burned at Baltimore on January 22, 1907. She had been built originally in 1903, at Bath, Maine.

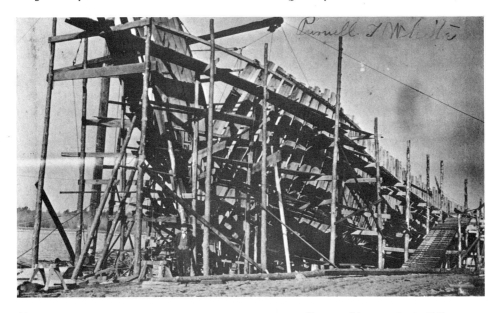

Alonzo R. Conley stands at the forefoot of the *Purnell T. White* on the building ways at Sharptown. Photo: John R. Conley

Miss Pauline White, sister of R. B. White and the schooner's namesake, was selected to christen the *Purnell T. White*. This was just the bare shell of a vessel. Unlike the launching of schooners in Maine, where many are fully rigged and some even have their sails bent so that they are ready to go to sea without any delay, the *Purnell T. White* did not even have her masts or bowsprit in position. But before she left the Nanticoke River she had been fitted with all her masts and spars complete with standing and running rigging. She lacked only her sails and these were bent later after she had left the builder's yard. In late fall of 1917, a tug arrived at Sharptown to tow the schooner away to commence her career at sea.

The *White* first appears in the 1918 issue of *Record of American and Foreign Shipping* and was classified A1 for 15 years, the highest rating given

Her hull complete, the schooner stands poised for launching. Photo: Joseph C. B. White

Alonzo R. Conley, designer and builder of the *Purnell T. White.* Mr. Conley was born at Sharptown on September 25, 1873, and died at Salisbury, Maryland, September 16, 1935. Photo: A. James Conley

to a new ship. To achieve this distinction she had to be built under the supervision of the American Bureau of Shipping. She carried this classification to the end of her sailing days. Additional information in the *Record* indicates that she was built of oak, yellow pine, hackmatack, fastened with galvanized iron fittings, and was salted.

Captain Fletcher Gantt was to have had command of the new schooner but, when launching was delayed, he took over another vessel. In Decem-

After her successful launching on August 22, 1917, the flag-bedecked *White* is taken in tow for the fitting-out dock at the Sharptown yard. Photo: Joseph C. B. White

Purnell Toadvine White, who bestowed his name upon the handsome four-masted schooner, was born at Shad Point, Maryland, on February 14, 1876, and died at Salisbury on May 16, 1948. Photo: Mrs. William P. Phillips

ber 1917, Captain William Ward, a 28-year-old native of Providence, Rhode Island, was appointed as master of the *White*. And the schooner's maiden voyage was to take her to the dark continent of Africa, one of the more distant ports of call for an American coasting schooner.

The first certificate of enrollment for the *Purnell T. White*, issued at Crisfield, Maryland, on October 22, 1917, indicated that the White Shipping

The new schooner is maneuvered to the shipyard dock where she will receive her spars and rigging. Photo: Joseph C. B. White

Company and its president, Albert W. Robinson, were sole owners of the schooner. On December 18, 1917, this enrollment was surrendered as the result of change in ownership and the new owners were listed as R. B. White, managing owner, of Salisbury, Maryland, with 50/161 parts; Albert W. Robinson, of Laurel, Delaware, 50/161; George W. Woolford of Cambridge, Maryland, 17/161; Alonzo R. Conley, 17/161; Purnell T. White,

17/161; and B. P. Gravenor of Sharptown, Maryland, 10/161. It is interesting to note how these owners were centered in the vicinity where the *Purnell T. White* was built and that most of them retained ownership for most of the life of the schooner. Albert W. Robinson was president of the Sharptown Bank, Sharptown; Purnell T. White was cashier of that bank and secretary and treasurer of the Sharptown Marine Railway Company; George W. Woolford was a businessman; Alonzo Conley was designer and builder of the ship; B. P. Gravenor was a sailmaker. Five of these men had vessels named for them. There were R. B. White and the three-masted schooner mentioned earlier. Albert W. Robinson gave his name to a four-masted schooner built at Sharptown in 1907. There was a sloop named *George W. Woolford* built at Cambridge in 1884 and the bugeye *Woolford* built the previous year at Madison, Maryland. In 1916 the ram *James H. Hargrave*, built at Sharptown in 1893, was renamed *B. P. Gravenor*. And, of course, there was *Purnell T. White*.*

Purnell T. White was chartered in February 1918, by John T. and Samuel H. Gillespie, Morristown, New Jersey, constituting the firm of L. C. Gillespie and Sons, to carry a general cargo "to the Belgian Congo on the west coast of Africa and return, stopping at Banana, Boma, and Matadi." Representative and attorney for the Gillespie firm was Fernand Verbeeck, general manager of a Belgian company in the Congo and in New York prior to the *White*'s departure from the latter port. He was given full power to attend to and oversee generally the discharging and loading of the schooner. According to the charter, Verbeeck was "to pay the captain of said vessel up to the sum of one thousand dollars out of any funds belonging to us that may be in the hands of our said attorney, and to purchase for us and on our account up to 5,000 pounds of ivory. . . ."

The *White* arrived in Africa "prior to May 30" and although she was scheduled to make several ports she only called at Boma. In the neighborhood of Matadi was the ill-famed Chaudron d'Enfer (Cauldron of Hell), a furious eddy water which made it quite impossible for a sailing vessel to negotiate. The facilities at Boma were rather primitive and discharging and loading had to be supervised by Captain Ward. This daily exposure to the Congo sun and heat proved to be detrimental to the health of the young shipmaster. He failed to heed Mr. Verbeeck's suggestions concerning care for himself in those latitudes. The *White* departed from Africa with a cargo of copal, a resin used in the manufacture of varnish, for the return passage to the United States. On July 19, Captain Ward died from malarial fever contracted at Boma. He was buried at sea the same day. He was the first of several masters to die while in command of that ship. Shortly after the schooner put into port upon completion of that voyage, her cook was found dead in the galley.

When the *White* set out on her second voyage, Captain Gantt had assumed command. Definite confirmation of the destination of the schooner's

---

* Names of owners of the *Purnell T. White* in later years appear in the Appendix.

Yachtlike in appearance and with a tug on her starboard side, the *White* passes through

Photo John P. Copley

second voyage has not been found. The New York Maritime Register did not list ship movements from July to December 1918. However, Miss Myrtle M. Gantt, the captain's daughter, seems to recall that this passage took the vessel to Teneriffe, Canary Islands. Then upon return to the States the schooner loaded a cargo of coal at Norfolk and on November 15 sailed for Para, Brazil, arriving there on December 13.

The *White* was in New York on October 17, 1918, for in the library of The Mariners Museum, in a group of original sketchbooks which belonged to the marine artist Antonio Jacobsen, there are 10 pages of rough drawings of the schooner prepared on that date at Gokey's Shipyard, Erie Basin. These were the basis for the schooner's portrait which serves as the frontispiece of this book. It is enlightening to see the effort that Jacobsen put into the sketches to record proper colors, location of fittings, and other details.

In the latter part of 1918, the War Trade Board ordered that no sailing vessels should leave Atlantic ports carrying foodstuffs, petroleum, rubber, or other materials which would be useful and of value to German U-boats that might capture them on the high seas. As a result, many vessels loaded with such cargoes and ready to depart were compelled to discharge. Exceptions in the application of the order were to be made of vessels that obviously, because of their destinations, would be unlikely to meet U-boats. In consequence of the new restriction, shippers diverted some of their sailing vessels to routes that did not cross the war areas. This may explain why the *Purnell T. White* did not cross the Atlantic again until after the Armistice.

On January 28, 1919, the schooner sailed from Para and arrived at New York on March 12. Then followed a most busy and successful career of a coasting schooner. Her cargoes were varied and her periods of idleness were few and of short duration. Much of this was apparently due to proper management. Her managing owner had a fleet of sailing vessels under his guidance, mostly two- and three-masters in the Chesapeake Bay trade, and they always seemed to have cargoes available.

It is most unusual that the entire career of a ship be preserved. The men in the C. C. Paul office must have been savers for when that office closed in the early 1950's, after it had been sold to Lloyd H. Lewis, a number of interesting records were found in the company safe. A notebook listed all the voyages made by the *Purnell T. White* from 1919 to the end of her active career in 1934, with dates of arrival and departure, and ports of call. In some instances, the cargoes she carried were mentioned. These usually consisted of bulk cargoes, like lumber, coal, salt, fish scrap, and logwood. Where the freights were not described, one could determine the cargoes without seeing them recorded, such as lumber from the Gulf and southeastern American ports, coal from New Jersey and Virginia, salt from Turks Island, and logwood from Haiti.

Purnell T. White at Boma, Belgian Congo, Africa, in March 1918, on her first voyage.
Photo: F. Verbeeck

Miss Pauline White with bouquet and christening bottle just prior to the launching of the schooner *Purnell T. White,* August 22, 1917. Photo: Mrs. William P. Phillips

Chapter 3

Voyages made by the schooner *Purnell T. White,* 1919–1934.

1919

April	12	Sailed from New York for Havre, France.*
May	19	Cable received May 19 from Havre, France.
June	15	Sailed from Havre for Halifax, Nova Scotia.
July	17	Arrived at Halifax.
August	14	Sailed from Halifax for Preston, England.
September	22	Arrived at Preston.
October	10	Cable from Liverpool — drydocking.
October	22	Cable from Liverpool, sailing for Haiti.

1920

January	3	Received telegram from Gulfport, Mississippi that vessel was proceeding to Mobile, Alabama.
January	8	Arrived at Mobile. After drydocking and making necessary repairs, vessel loaded 621M feet of lumber for San Juan, Puerto Rico
March	19	Sailed for San Juan.
April	20	Cable from San Juan announcing arrival. Delayed at San Juan account of strike.
June	21	Cable from San Juan announcing sailing for Miragoane, Haiti (sailed June 16).
June	28	Cable announcing arrival at Miragoane (arrived June 23).
July	13	Cable announcing sailing from Miragoane for Baltimore.
July	24	Arrived at Baltimore.
August	30	Sailed from Baltimore for Havana, Cuba.
September	25	Cable from Havana announcing arrival (delayed account congestion at Havana).
November	9	Sailed for Tampa, Florida.
November	14	Arrived at Tampa.

1921

January	20	Sailed for Cienfugos, Cuba (in command of Captain W. S. Saunders).
January	31	Cable from Cienfugos announcing arrival.

---

* 3,925 barrels of oil at $12.00 per barrel freight.

March	5	Sailed for Georgetown, South Carolina.
March	21	Arrived at Georgetown.
April	23	Sailed from Georgetown for New York.
May	10	Arrived at New York. After discharging, hauled for copper painting, etc., at Perth Amboy, New Jersey.
June	14	Sailed June 14 for Wilmington, North Carolina, with coal.
June	21	Arrived at Wilmington.
June	29	Sailed from Wilmington for Georgetown.
July	6	Arrived at Georgetown.
July	19	Sailed from Georgetown for New York.
July	24	Arrived at New York.
August	18	Sailed from New York for Georgetown.
August	24	Arrived at Georgetown.
September	12	Sailed for New York.
September	17	Arrived at New York
October	4	Left New York in tow for Philadelphia, 5 P.M.
October	6	Arrived at Philadelphia, 4 P.M.
October	15	Sailed for Martinique. Cable from Martinique, November 14, Captain W. S. Saunders ill; Captain H. T. Hansen left on the S. S. *Guiana* from New York for Martinique, December 14, 1921. Cable from Captain Hansen from Martinique, December 30, 1921, stating vessel was sailing for Turks Island. Also, Captain Saunders and mate, George F. Lowe, were sailing for New York on S. S. *Guiana*. Captain and mate arrived in New York, January 6, 1922.

1922

January	16	Cable from Turks Island announcing arrival.
January	22	Cable from Turks Island, sailing for Baltimore.
February	15	Arrived at Baltimore.
March	30	Sailed from Baltimore for Nassau. In command Captain Fletcher M. Gantt.
April	10	Cable from Nassau.
April	13	Sailed for Kilkenny, Georgia.
April	16	Arrived at Brunswick Bar.
April	20	Arrived at Kilkenny.
May	4	Sailed for New York.
May	10	Arrived at New York.
May	27	Sailed for Baltimore.
June	14	Arrived at Baltimore.
June	22	Sailed for Nassau.
August	6	Cable from consignees to shippers advising arrival. Also stating illness of Captain Gantt. Captain Gantt died August 10, at night. Captain L. S. Tawes sailed August 11 on steamer to take charge.
August	17	Cable, sailing for Baltimore.
August	26	Arrived at Baltimore.

September 23	Left Baltimore, in command of Captain George E. Fleming, for Reedville, Virginia, to load (fish) scrap for Portland, Connecticut.
September 27	Sailed for Portland. Cargo fired October 2. Discharged cargo at Norfolk.
October	7	Sailed for Bucksport, Maine.
October	14	Sailed from Bucksport for Brighton, Trinidad.
November	23	Arrived at Trinidad.
December	2	Sailed for Aruba.
December	5	Arrived at Aruba.
December	21	Sailed for Charleston, South Carolina.

1923

January	7	Arrived Charleston.
January	27	Sailed from Charleston for Turks Island.
February	2	Arrived Turks Island.
February	7	Sailed from Turks Island for Baltimore.
March	3	Arrived Baltimore.
April	6	Sailed from Baltimore for Georgetown.
April	16	Arrived Georgetown.
May	1	Sailed from Georgetown for Baltimore.
May	12	Arrived Baltimore.
June	8	Sailed from Baltimore for Martinique.
July	3	Arrived Martinique.
July	30	Sailed for Turks Island.
August	4	Arrived at Turks Island.
August	10	Sailed from Turks Island for Portland Maine.
August	31	Arrived Portland.
September	17	Sailed from Portland for Somes Sound, Maine.
September	18	At Somes Sound.
September	29	Sailed from Somes Sound for New York.
October	13	Arrived New York.
October	26	Sailed from New York for Georgetown.
November	4	Arrived Georgetown.
November	23	Sailed from Georgetown for New York.
December	3	Arrived at New York. Finished discharging at Stamford, Connecticut.

1924

January	15	Sailed from New York for Turks Island.
February	5	Arrived Turks Island.
February	22	Sailed from Turks Island for Baltimore.
April	4	Arrived at Baltimore.
April	29	Left Baltimore at 6 P.M. in tow of tug *Mary Clare* for Little Choptank River, Maryland. Arrived April 30.
May	21	Left Choptank for San Juan, Puerto Rico.
June	20	At San Juan.

July	5	Sailed for Monte Cristi, Haiti.
July	7	At Monte Cristi.
August	16	Sailed from Monte Cristi for Philadelphia.
September	3	Arrived Philadelphia.
September	25	Sailed from Philadelphia for Martinique.
October	28	Cable from Martinique.
November	17	Cable from Martinique sailing for Turks Island.
November	25	Cable, arrival at Turks Island.
November	30	Cable from Turks Island, sailing for Baltimore.
December	13	At Baltimore.

1925

February	19	Sailed for Jacksonville.
March	3	At Jacksonville.
March	13	Sailed for Havana, Cuba.
March	26	At Havana.
April	6	Sailed from Havana for Georgetown, South Carolina.
April	17	At Georgetown.
April	30	Sailed from Georgetown for Mayaguez, Puerto Rico.
May	21	Cable from Mayaguez.
June	–	Sailed for St. Marc, Haiti.
June	13	At St. Marc.
June	29	Sailed from St. Marc for Camden, New Jersey.
July	14	At Camden.
July	29	Sailed from Philadelphia for St. John, New Brunswick.
August	19	At St. John.
August	28	Sailed from St. John for Halifax, Nova Scotia.
September	3	At Halifax.
October	2	Sailed for New York.
October	31	At New York.
November	17	Sailed from New York for Miami.
December	3	At Miami.

1926

January	7	Sailed from Miami for Mobile.
January	–	At Mobile.
February	5	Sailed from Mobile for Miami.
February	13	Arrived at Miami.
March	16	Sailed from Miami for Monte Cristi.
April	4	Arrived at Monte Cristi.
April	17	Cable, sailing from Monte Cristi for Philadelphia.
May	13	At Philadelphia.
May	26	Sailed from Philadelphia for Darien, Georgia.
June	9	Arrived at Darien.
June	24	Sailed from Darien for Philadelphia.
July	7	Arrived at Philadelphia.
July	22	Sailed from Philadelphia for Norfolk, Virginia.

July	28	Arrived at Norfolk.
August	10	Sailed from Norfolk for Bermuda.
August	18	Arrived at Bermuda.
August	25	Sailed from Bermuda for St. Marc, Haiti.
October	6	Arrived at St. Marc.
October	14	Sailed from St. Marc for Baltimore. Picked up by revenue cutter, November 3, with sails blown away account encountering hurricane and taken into Cape Lookout, North Carolina. Towed from Cape Lookout, November 6, by tug *Barrenfork* to Baltimore.
November	8	Arrived at Baltimore.
December	15	Sailed from Baltimore for Point à Pitre, Guadeloupe.

1927

January	20	Arrived at Point à Pitre.
February	8	Sailed from Point à Pitre for Gonaives, Haiti.
February	15	Cable, arrived Gonaives.
March	5	Sailed from Gonaives for Newport News, Virginia.
March	21	Arrived Newport News.
April	12	Sailed from Newport News for Georgetown.
April	16	Arrived at Georgetown.
April	30	Sailed from Georgetown for New York.
May	11	Arrived at New York.
May	23	Towed from New York to Bridgeport, Connecticut.
May	26	Arrived at Bridgeport.
June	4	Sailed from Bridgeport for Cabo Rojo, Puerto Rico.
July	2	Arrived at Cabo Rojo.
July	20	Sailed from Cabo Rojo for New York.
August	3	Arrived at New York. Captain Nicklas relieved by Captain A. S. Wallace at New York, August 8.
August	30	Sailed from New York for St. Marc, Haiti.
October	4	Arrived at St. Marc.
October	18	Sailed from St. Marc for Baltimore.
November	8	Arrived at Baltimore.
December	17	Sailed from Baltimore for Newport News.
December	22	Arrived at Newport News.
December	31	Sailed from Newport News for Hamilton, Bermuda.

1928

January	8	Arrived Hamilton.
January	16	Sailed from Hamilton for Port au Prince, Haiti.
January	30	Arrived Port au Prince.
February	18	Sailed from Port au Prince for Baltimore.
March	7	Passed in Virginia capes 4:30 P.M.
March	10	Arrived at Baltimore.
March	21	Sailed from Baltimore for Jacksonville.
April	6	Arrived at Jacksonville.

April	22	Sailed from Jacksonville for New York.
April	30	Arrived at New York.
May	26	Sailed from New York for Palatka, Florida.
June	27	Arrived at Palatka.
July	12	Sailed from Jacksonville for New York.
July	20	Arrived at New York.
August	25	Sailed from New York for Jacksonville.
September	10	Arrived at Jacksonville.
October	9	Sailed from Jacksonville for New York.
October	23	Arrived at New York.
November	23	Sailed from New York for Georgetown.
December	3	Arrived at Georgetown.
December	18	Sailed from Georgetown for Baltimore.

1929

January	1	Arrived at Baltimore.
January	12	Sailed from Baltimore for Georgetown.
January	26	Arrived at Georgetown.
February	10	Sailed from Georgetown for Baltimore.
February	26	Arrived at Baltimore.
March	16	Sailed from Baltimore for Georgetown.
March	28	Arrived at Georgetown.
April	16	Sailed from Georgetown for Baltimore.
April	21	Arrived at Baltimore.
May	18	Sailed from Baltimore for Georgetown.
May	23	Arrived at Georgetown.
June	18	Sailed from Georgetown for Baltimore.
June	25	Arrived at Baltimore.
July	9	Sailed from Baltimore for Georgetown.
August	6	Arrived at Georgetown.
August	22	Sailed from Georgetown for Baltimore.
August	30	Arrived at Baltimore.
September	18	Sailed from Baltimore for Georgetown. Went ashore October 2, at Cape Lookout Bight. Floated October 14 by revenue cutter and taken to Southport, North Carolina, and then towed to Georgetown.
October	16	Arrived at Georgetown.
October	27	Sailed from Georgetown for Baltimore.
November	6	Arrived at Baltimore.
November	19	Sailed from Baltimore for Georgetown.
November	28	Arrived at Georgetown.
December	15	Sailed from Georgetown for Baltimore.
December	26	Arrived at Baltimore.

1930

| January | 11 | Sailed from Baltimore for Georgetown. |
| January | 21 | Arrived at Georgetown. |

February	6	Sailed from Georgetown for Baltimore.
February	13	Arrived at Baltimore.
February	26	Sailed from Baltimore for Georgetown.
March	24	Arrived at Georgetown.
April	13	Sailed from Georgetown for Baltimore.
April	23	Arrived at Baltimore.
May	9	Sailed from Baltimore for Georgetown.
May	24	Arrived at Georgetown.
June	17	Sailed from Georgetown for Baltimore.
June	22	Arrived at Baltimore.
July	9	Sailed from Baltimore for Georgetown.
August	1	Arrived at Georgetown.
August	15	Sailed from Georgetown for Baltimore.
September	3	Arrived at Baltimore.
September	20	Sailed from Baltimore for Georgetown.
October	2	Arrived at Georgetown.
October	14	Sailed from Georgetown for Baltimore.
October	26	Arrived at Baltimore.
November	10	Towed from Baltimore for Norfolk.
November	16	Towed below Thimble Shoal Light (Va.).
November	22	Passed out Cape Henry with cement bound for Georgetown. On December 29, was advised by Radio Corporation of America that S. S. *W. H. Doheny* (Captain Spurr) spoke schooner *Purnell T. White* at 7 A.M., December 25, 89 miles north of San Salvador steering west for Hole in Wall (Bahamas). Reported off Florida coast December 29.

1931

January	2	Towed into Fernandina, Florida, by revenue cutter.
January	–	Sailed from Fernandina for Georgetown.
January	9	Arrived at Georgetown.
February	7	Sailed from Georgetown for Baltimore.
February	19	Arrived at Baltimore.
March	4	Sailed from Baltimore for Georgetown.
March	14	Arrived at Georgetown.
March	29	Sailed from Georgetown for Baltimore.
April	8	Arrived at Baltimore.
April	23	Discharged. Shifted to Woodall's (shipyard at Baltimore) to be tied up, May 8.
November	11	Sailed from Baltimore for Georgetown.
December	1	Arrived at Georgetown.
December	10?	Sailed from Georgetown for Baltimore. Passed in Cape Henry 2 P.M., December 14.
December	18	Arrived at Baltimore. Discharged January 29.

1932

March	1	Sailed from Baltimore for Georgetown.

March	7	Arrived off bar at Georgetown.
March	21	Sailed from Georgetown for Baltimore.
March	31	Arrived at Baltimore. Discharged April 15.
December	3	Sailed from Pier 8, Baltimore, for Georgetown.
December	18	Arrived at Georgetown.

1933

January	4	Sailed from Georgetown, 6 P.M., for New York.
January	13	Arrived at New York (outside Sandy Hook, January 12).
February	2	Discharged.
February	17	Sailed from New York for Georgetown.
March	1	Arrived at Georgetown.
March	21	Sailed from Georgetown for Baltimore.
April	3	Arrived at Baltimore. Discharged April 24.
June	6	Sailed from Baltimore for Georgetown.
June	17	Arrived at Georgetown.
July	2	Sailed from Georgetown for New York.
July	20	Arrived at New York.
August	9	Sailed from New York for Georgetown.
August	21	Arrived at Georgetown.
September	23	Sailed from Georgetown for New York.
October	4	Arrived at New York.
October	23	Sailed from New York for Georgetown.
October	28	Arrived at Georgetown.
November	19	Sailed from Georgetown for New York.
December	2	Arrived at New York.

1934

January	3	Sailed from New York for Georgetown.
January	11	Arrived at Georgetown.
January	27	Sailed from Georgetown for New York. On February 7, reported 200 miles east of Cape Fear by S. S. *Maiden Creek*, sails gone and running low in provisions, asking for assistance. Two revenue cutters sent for her and picked her up at 2:15 P.M. and taking her into Hampton Roads. Later reported 65 miles southeast of Cape Henry, waterlogged with cutter *Mendota* holding her, hove to. Vessel lost February 9, about sundown. Captain Nicklas, mate, cook Jim Lee, and one sailor lost. Three sailors rescued by revenue cutter and taken to Norfolk, arriving morning of February 10.

Chapter 4

THE listing of a ship's voyages can be a casual, statistical affair. Most of the entries on the preceding pages appear to have been routine and devoid of mishaps or excitement. If the logbooks of the *Purnell T. White* existed, their notations probably would reveal many events that could befall any seaworthy, well-managed ship. In 1919 the schooner voyaged to Preston, England. That she was buffeted by heavy seas is evident in a photograph taken on that trip showing a portion of her taffrail, stern davits, and yawl boat torn away. However, no written description of her encounter with this storm has been found.

The entry for the *White* sailing from Turks Island, Bahamas, on February 22, 1924, for Baltimore and arriving at her destination on April 4 does not indicate anything other than that the passage was longer than might be anticipated. She had on board a cargo of salt consigned to Charles M. Struven and Company. The four-masted schooner *Charles M. Struven*, which left Turks Island for Baltimore five days before the departure of the *White*, had passed in Cape Henry within fifteen days.

For more than a month Coast Guard and merchant vessels were on the lookout for the *White*. It was feared that she had gone down as a result of the heavy gales which swept the east coast on March 11–12 causing the loss of the steamer *Santiago* and six-masted schooner *Wyoming*. First word of the schooner came from the Norwegian steamer *John Blumer* when she docked at New York and reported that on March 25 she spoke the *White* 300 miles off Jacksonville, Florida, and supplied her with provisions. In early April the schooner, flying distress signals, was sighted by a lookout at the Dam Neck Mills Coast Guard station, south of Virginia Beach. She was about five miles east-southeast of the station and was slowly making her way to the mouth of Chesapeake Bay. Unable to send a surfboat out to the stricken vessel because of rough seas, the station reported her plight to the Norfolk Coast Guard base. The cutter *Mascoutin* was dispatched to her aid and brought her into Hampton Roads for anchorage. It was reported that her sails had been damaged and her windlass was inoperative. A Norfolk tug was chartered to tow the schooner to Baltimore where her master, Captain George E. Fleming, of Dover, New Hampshire, told of battling gales that drove him far to sea.

In 1925-26 the Miami building boom was at its height. The need for materials offered many large schooners and other sailing ships the opportunity to secure charters. This was the last large gathering of active sailing ships along the east coast. The *White* made two passages there with lumber the latter part of 1925 and in early 1926.

On August 25, 1926, the *White* left Bermuda for St. Marc, Haiti, to load logwood for Baltimore. As the voyage extended into weeks, fear was felt for her safety. On October 6, the schooner reached St. Marc and her master, Captain Charles Nicklas, told of experiencing two hurricanes on his 41-day passage. She left Haiti on October 14 and encountered another hurricane which disabled her. On November 1, she was sighted fourteen miles northeast of Cape Lookout as she made her way to Morehead City, North Carolina. The Coast Guard cutter *Modoc* went to her aid and brought her into port where her crew related their battle with the storm, torn sails, leaks, and exhaustion of food. On November 6, she was taken in tow for Baltimore by the tug *Barrenfork* and arrived there two days later.

While bound from Halifax, Nova Scotia, to Preston, England, August-September 1919, the *White* encountered heavy weather which carried away part of her taffrail, stern davits, and yawl boat. Her master, Captain Fletcher M. Gantt, leans against the taffrail.
Photo: Miss Myrtle M. Gantt

The *White* ranged far and wide off the eastern seaboard during her career but in January 1928 she made her last foreign landfall, to Port au Prince, Haiti. The latter part of that year she started the series of passages from New York or Baltimore to Georgetown, South Carolina. Except for one instance, that was to be a rather steady trade for the next five years.

Her stranding in September 1929, at Cape Lookout Bight was a near disaster. She remained aground in that exposed position, after loss of her two anchors, for almost two weeks but was finally floated free and towed to safety. Her only damage was the loss of a portion of her forefoot which interfered with her sailing abilities later on. She was fortunate to have been released from the sands of that dreaded North Carolina coast.

Captain Fletcher M. Gantt on the quarterdeck of the *Purnell T. White* at sea.
Photo: Miss Myrtle M. Gantt

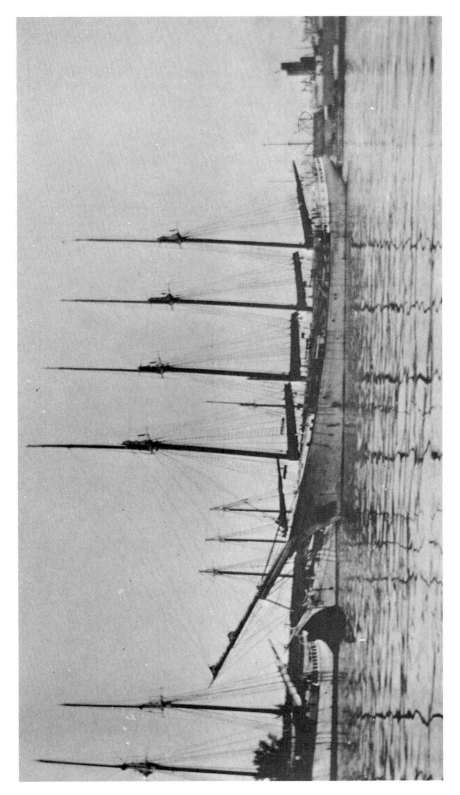

Purnell T. White at Miami, Florida, with a cargo of lumber in 1926.
Photo: William L. Earll

The distance by sea between Norfolk, Virginia, and Georgetown, South Carolina, is a little over 400 miles. In the latter part of 1930, the *White* departed from that Virginia port with a cargo of cement consigned to Georgtown. Almost two months were to elapse before she arrived at her destination due to being blown far off her course down to the Bahamas.

On that occasion the schooner had first been towed into Fernandina, Florida, by a Coast Guard cutter before continuing her passage to Georgetown. At Fernandina, newspaper reporters interviewed her master, Captain Charles Nicklas, and he gave the following account of the heavy weather which prolonged his voyage.

"We were off the Virginia capes when a gale lashed the schooner off her course. For days the vessel wallowed in the seas and we spread oil to keep them from breaking over our decks. There were lulls, some for a whole day at a time, before another cross gale would shift her far from her course. Every drop of oil, except what was actually needed for the lights and other necessities, was put overboard from the two canvas buckets on either side of her bow. The waves were thirty feet high. Our food and water supply began to run low. We caught enough rain water, however, to keep us from thirst.

"Then one of the men became ill of a fever. I thought every day that the sailor would die and I would have to sew him in canvas and send him overboard, but he made it and is now up and doing his work with the rest of them. They had to save the best food for the sick man—the canned soup and the 'bully beef tea,' but they had some canned beef and flour and water on which to subsist.

"Then there was the radio. The men rigged it up with a battery from one of the hoisting engines. For the life of me, I could not get a weather report through. Every time I would try there would be some musical program or other entertainment. I never expect to see any continually rougher weather than I have had the past forty-odd days."

The *Purnell T. White* might be considered a typical coasting schooner relative to the cargoes she carried and the ports visited. However, she was above average in her steady employment. Some of the vessels of the Boston-owned, Crowell and Thurlow fleet were tied up for years due to lack of charters. But the *White* was never to suffer long periods of idleness. The depression of the early 1930's hit her as it did all shipping. In May 1931, she was tied up in Baltimore after discharging a cargo of Georgetown lumber and was inactive until the following November. The next year she was laid up in April and tugged at her mooring lines in Baltimore harbor until December. Then she went to sea again and plied a steady trade with lumber out of Georgtown for Baltimore or New York.

The longest period of idleness for the *White* was from April to December, 1932. Here she is tied up at Pier 8, President Street, Baltimore, on September 23 of that year. The motor yawl boat can be seen slung from her stern davits. Photo: Author

Chapter 5

ON ONE of her passages from New York to Georgetown, in October 1933, James S. McCullough signed on the *White*. He was a typical merchant seaman of that period, out of a job like so many of his shipmates during the depression years but, unlike them, he seemed to prefer sailing ships to steamers. He had previously sailed in the schooners *Annie M. Murphy, Cumberland Queen* (and after she was renamed *Emerett*), *Edwin G. Farrar, Virginia Pendleton,* and *Albert F. Paul*; barkentines *John C. Meyer, Prins Valdemar,* and *City of Beaumont;* and full-rigged ship *Sophie*. He was also unlike the average seaman of those days in that he was more observant and kept journals of some of those voyages and took photographs on board. But much of that material "was lost in flooded fo'c'sles, lost seabags, torpedoed ships, and flooded cellars."

What he did preserve or salvage resulted in a most interesting account of his round-trip on the *Purnell T. White* in 1933. This is about the most detailed record of any coasting schooner voyage and reveals the on-board-at-sea activities of that vessel.

Mr. McCullough eventually went into steam as his sea career progressed and in 1965 he was mate on an oil tanker operating in the Korean area. He came home to New York that summer and died while on leave. Through the kindness of his wife, the account of her husband's 1933 trip in the *Purnell T. White* follows.

The usual crowd of sailing ship men were standing around the corner of Coenties Slip and South Street, New York City, on October 18, 1933. The shipping master, a short, fat, red-faced man about fifty years old, walked up.

"I want four men for the *Purnell T. White*," said he.

"Where's she going?" asked one of the men.

"Georgetown, South Carolina, and back."

"What does she pay?"

"Thirty dollars."

"It ain't enough," said the crowd.

"Times are hard and that's all she can afford to pay," replied the shipping master. "Do you want the job?"

"All right," said one. "It's a chance to get off the beach."

"How about you?"

The *White* is towed out of New York harbor, circa 1930, with an assist from her lower sails. Photo: John A. Noble

"Oh, I suppose so. There ain't nothing else."
"And you?"
"No sir, none of those coffins for me."

Well, anyway, the shipping master got four men to agree to ship in her, I being one of them, and the final instructions were, "Be at Swan's (a ship chandler) tomorrow morning with your bags and sign on. You can go aboard with the stores. The vessel is lying at Gates Lumber Yard on East River."

The next day the crew for the schooner *White* stood around in front of the ship chandler's store waiting for the shipping master to come along with the ship's articles. He showed up about 10 o'clock, all out of breath and his hand full of important looking papers.

"All right, boys, come on in here and sign articles. No use to read them to you. You know what they are. Georgetown and pay off north of Hatteras, thirty dollars a month." He handed the pen to the nearest man. The man, with an awkward and trembling hand (not from fright but from too much rum) wrote Andrew Johnson.

"All right, Johnson, where were you born?" asked the shipping master.

"Norway."

"Citizen?"

"Well, I've been here long enough to be one."

"How old are you?"

"Fifty-four."

"You've been fifty-four for the last ten years. How tall are you?"

"Five foot eight."

"Eyes—blue. Hair? Take off your cap. Well, you ain't got much, but it's grey. What's your address?"

"25 South Street."

"All right; next man," and so on until we all had signed on.

"Now," said the shipping master, "the truck ain't here yet but put your bags over there with the ship's stores and I'll give you carfare so you can go aboard and get your dinner. The cook and mate are aboard. Take the Fourth Avenue Express to 125th street, transfer to the Hunt's Point local and get off at 149th Street. Walk down toward the river and you'll see the vessel. She's the only schooner at the dock." He handed us twenty cents and said, "Don't forget me when you get back, boys." He had a speakeasy. "So long, boys. You'll have a good trip. She's a good vessel and it'll be nice and warm down south."

We boarded the subway at Bowling Green and in due time arrived at 149th Street. From there we had no difficulty in finding the vessel.

The *Purnell T. White* was a four-masted schooner (wooden) of 688 net tons and hailed from Salisbury, Maryland. She was built at Sharptown, Maryland, in 1917, and operated by C. C. Paul and Company of Baltimore. A fine looking vessel (for a schooner) with plenty of sheer and more rake to the masts than most schooners. The hull was painted grey outside. The cabin trunk, deckhouses, rails, and inside of bulwarks were white; the waterways dark green; booms and gaffs mast color (buff); crosstrees and blocks aloft white, and the decks oiled with pine oil. She looked like a down-east built vessel, everything handy and plenty of room on deck.

The mate met us at the gangway. He was a big fellow about forty years old and looked more like a farmer than a sailor. "Well, I suppose you're the

After the towing hawser is released, the schooner sets her headsails. Photo: John A. Noble

new crew," said he. "There is some gasoline (used to run the pump and donkey engines) on the dock. Let's get it aboard before dinner."

"We ain't got our working clothes. They're coming down with the stores," Johnson answered.

"Oh, I thought those were your working clothes," said the mate sarcastically. "You can't hurt them, anyway." So we took aboard 100 gallons of gasoline which filled up the tanks.

"All right, men, get your dinner." And we went into the forecastle.

The forecastle was in the forward end of the deckhouse, on the port side. It was about 9 by 10 feet. There was a sliding door toward the after end on the port side, and a square port lighted the place. Two double-decked, fore and aft, bunks running from the forward bulkhead on each side, a bench

Upper and lower bunks on the forward, starboard bulkhead of the forecastle, where the seamen quartered, on the *Purnell T. White*. These consisted of lockers beneath the lower bunk, a bench, and cheap, straw-filled mattresses known as "donkey breakfasts" covering the hard board bunks. Photo: Dwight Foster

secured to each lower bunk, and a little table two feet square fastened to the after bulkhead, made up the furniture of the place. It had been newly painted white and grey and was a better forecastle than is usually found on east coast schooners.

"Well," said old John as he sat down and lit his pipe, "if I had a nickel I'd go back to South Street. I kin see this mate is no dam' good."

"What about your clothes?" asked Andy. "You'd lose 'em."

"Oh, they're nothing but rags, except the boots. That's all I got out of my last payday."

"Well, that's pretty good for you, ain't it?"

About that time the cook, whom we could hear rattling his pots and pans in the galley, shoved back the slide of the pie hole which opened onto the little table and passed in some tin plates, cups, knives, forks, and spoons. "There," said he, "is your mess gear. Take good care of it 'cause there ain't no more." We each picked out a set and put it in the bunk we were going to occupy. "Come and get it," sang out the cook as he started to pass the grub through the pie hole: a platter of roast beef, a big pan of boiled

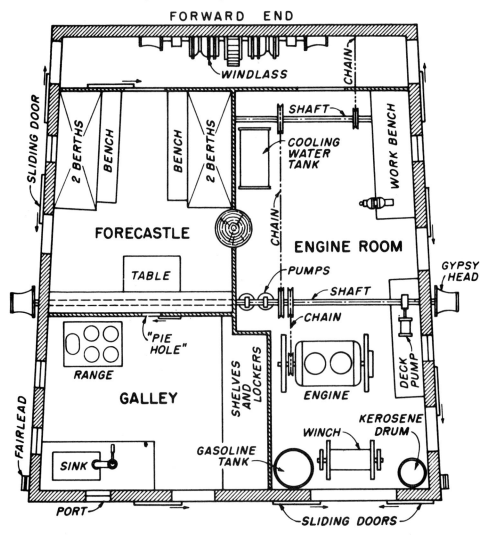

Layout of the forward house of the *Purnell T. White*. The drawing was developed from pencil sketches made aboard the schooner by James S. McCullough in 1933.
Courtesy: *Nautical Research Journal*

potatoes, a plate heaped high with homemade bread, a big pot of hot coffee, a little dish of butter, a pound or so of sugar in a coffee can, and a can of sweetened, condensed milk.

"Well, one thing sure," said Nick, "she feeds good and plenty," and he started to fill up his plate. The rest of us followed his example, then with

44

plates on our knees, cups on deck in front of us, we sat on the benches and ate our dinner. After the meal each man took a piece of bread and wiped out his plate and put it away. The platter, pans, and coffee pot were passed back to the cook who then informed us that we would get our blankets from the captain after supper. There was a donkey's breakfast (cheap mattress) and pillow, not very clean, in each bunk.

The truck arrived with the stores and our seabags. We changed our clothes and went to work getting the stores aboard; salt and fresh meat, potatoes, cabbage, carrots, onions, salt fish, canned goods, eggs, butter, coffee, etc.; paint—white, green, black, red, and buff; Stockholm tar for the rigging, pine oil for the decks, yards of duck to patch sails, spun yarn,

Captain Charles Nicklas (third from left) on board the *Purnell T. White* at Miami, Florida, December 1925. Photo: William L. Earll

marline, ratline stuff, sail twine, marlinspikes, charts, red bunting for a new wind sock, coils of rope, etc. All this was stored in its proper place: fresh meat in the ice chest, vegetables in the potato locker, paint, tar, oil, salt meat and fish in the forward lazarette, canvas under the mate's bunk, and so on until everything was stored away properly. Next, a truck came alongside with 1,500 pounds of ice which went into the ice chest built alongside the pantry in the cabin. It was supper time by then but a truck came alongside with a ton of coal to be taken aboard. It was stowed in the usual but most inconvenient place, down the forward lazarette hatch into the alleyway between the cabin trunk and ship's side.

That over, we went forward to our supper of beef stew, bread, and tea. The tea wasn't much as a beverage but it was hot, therefore excellent for cleaning the grease off the plates. The procedure was to pour a little tea in

45

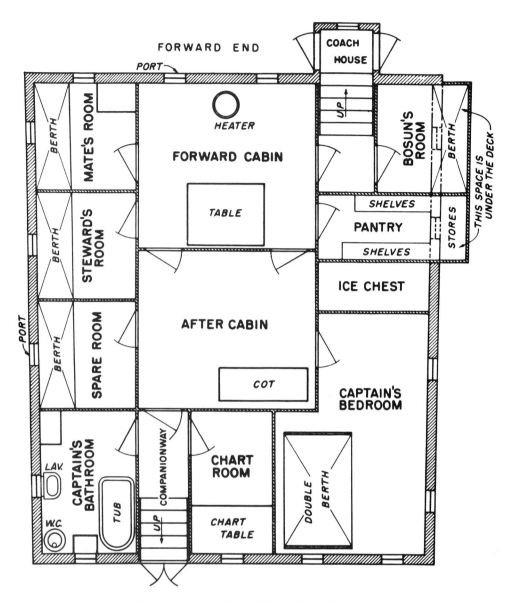

FORWARD END

PORT

COACH HOUSE

HEATER

FORWARD CABIN

TABLE

BERTH

MATE'S ROOM

BERTH

STEWARD'S ROOM

BERTH

SPARE ROOM

PORT

UP

BOSUN'S ROOM

BERTH

THIS SPACE IS UNDER THE DECK

SHELVES

PANTRY

SHELVES

STORES

ICE CHEST

AFTER CABIN

COT

CAPTAIN'S BEDROOM

LAV.

CAPTAIN'S BATHROOM

TUB

W.C.

UP

COMPANIONWAY

CHART ROOM

CHART TABLE

DOUBLE BERTH

The after house or cabin trunk of the *Purnell T. White* where the captain, mate, bo'sun, and cook lived and ate their meals. Courtesy: *Nautical Research Journal*

the plate, wash it around until the grease was pretty well off, then empty it overboard. Plates cleaned, we filled them with stew and sat down on the benches to enjoy our evening meal. After supper, if there was any tea left the plates usually got another cleaning. Coffee was rarely used to clean plates as it was a popular beverage and very seldom was any left from a meal. The mess kits were sent back to the galley and after having a smoke we went aft to get our blankets from the skipper.

The captain, Charles Nicklas, was a tall, thin, square-shouldered man, somewhat stooped and a little faltering as he was over seventy years old. He

On the voyage from New York City to Georgetown, South Carolina, in October 1933, the *Purnell T. White* runs before the wind wing-and-wing with topsails clewed up.
Photo: J. S. McCullough

was smooth shaven with high cheek bones, a rather prominent Roman nose, grey, deep set eyes, sparse grey hair, and a wrinkled, weather beaten complexion. Later we were to learn that he was one of the finest men to sail with on the coast. He did not believe in carrying sail too long nor did he expect the crew to do a lot of unnecessary work at sea—quite different from the mate who did not know how to handle sail and once said, "No one will have it easy as long as I am mate aboard this vessel."

The skipper gave us our blankets, two for each man, and while they were of poor quality they were clean.

It was quite chilly that October evening and as we had no stove in the forecastle we soon put out the light and turned in for the night, fairly well satisfied with the vessel but not the mate.

We were awakened about 6:30 A.M. on October 20 by the rattle of pots and pans in the galley. A quick wash in a bucket of cold water on deck and we were ready for our breakfast. "I guess there ain't no bed bugs in this packet," said Andy, "but maybe it's too cold for them to come out."

"Well, she's sure full of cockroaches," said Nick, "and where there's plenty of cockroaches you don't find many bed bugs."

"Come and get it," sang out the cook as he pushed back the slide of the pie hole and passed in a pan of oatmeal with milk already in it, a platter of ham and eggs, not very much ham and one egg for each man (but that's all a sailor ever gets on any vessel if he gets eggs at all), a pan of boiled potatoes, plenty of bread, and a pot of hot coffee. Breakfast over, we sat down to have a smoke, but not for long. Promptly at 8 o'clock the mate appeared in the doorway with his cheery, "Turn to, men."

The tug would be alongside at high water to tow us out to sea if the wind was fair, or to an anchorage inside of Sandy Hook if the wind was ahead. We had plenty to do to get the vessel ready for sea. The towing hawser was broken out and coiled down on the forecastlehead; jib sheets rove off, then the fore, main, mizzen, and spanker sheets; halliards thrown down from the sheer poles and coiled in the waterways; dunnage in the hold piled up alongside the keelson and secured to keep it from going adrift if the vessel rolled at sea; and finally the strongbacks and hatches were put on. We had just finished that job when the towboat *John B. Caddell* came alongside. We took enough fresh water from her to fill our tanks, singled up our mooring lines, and at noon, high water, we passed the towing hawser to the tug and let go the remaining mooring lines. A man went to the wheel and we were on our way down the East River.

After dinner the fenders and mooring lines were stowed in the hold, the pump rigged, and the vessel was washed down fore and aft. When we got down into the lower bay the wind was about east, head wind, so the tug steamed over toward an anchorage on West Bank. When the vessel arrived in a favorable position the towboat reduced speed, swung around, and gave us a signal on her whistle to heave in the towing hawser. The mate stood by on the forecastlehead waiting for an order from the captain to let go the anchor. The captain stood by the rail on the poop deck looking over the side watching the movement of the vessel through the water. As soon as the vessel lost headway he gave the order, "Let go the starboard anchor." "Let go the starboard anchor," repeated the mate, and one of the sailors released the windlass compressor. The anchor went down with a splash, rumble, and roar. "Forty-five fathoms outside the hawse pipe," shouted the skipper. "Forty-five fathoms, Sir," repeated the mate.

It was about 3 P.M. when we anchored. The vessel was ready for sea so the mate put all hands to cutting wood for the cook until 4 P.M. Then he knocked us, off. As we went into the forecastle, John said, "The dollars are coming in through the hawse pipe now." I think all hands would rather have had a fair wind and set sail, for one might as well be a thousand miles out to sea as anchored off Sandy Hook. We spent the hour before supper getting things in the forecastle arranged and secured for a two-month trip. After supper the anchor lights were trimmed and run up.

A few minutes before 8 P.M. the mate came forward. "Anchor watch, men," he said, "call me and the captain if the wind goes around anywhere from north to sou'west. If it breezes up and she takes anymore chain let me know. One man on watch at a time will be enough. Mind the anchor lights don't go out and if it gets thick ring the bell. Call me and the cook at four o'clock. John, you and Nick will be on the Old Man's watch and you two fellows will be on my watch. Split up the anchor watch to suit yourselves. Keep up a good lookout. There's lots of traffic around here." That said, the mate went aft.

The anchor watch lasted from 8 P.M. until 4 A.M., two hours apiece. To settle the matter as to who was to get the first, second, and third watches we drew matchsticks, the shortest stick taking the first watch, etc. Despite all the instructions the mate gave us, standing anchor watch is quite simple and it's seldom that anyone calls the afterguard even if the wind goes around fair. If someone from aft comes on deck unexpectedly and finds the wind blowing fair, tell him it has just shifted or has been baffling and you were just waiting to see if it was going to be steady. No one but the skipper likes to be aroused out of a warm bunk to get under way on a cold dark night.

The last man on watch called the mate at 4 A.M. and turned in. At 5 A.M. the mate shoved open the forecastle door and called out, "All hands, turn out to get under way." We rolled out of our bunks, dressed, and went out on deck to find it calm with an occasional light air from the north'ard, not enough to set sail, so we stood around until seven bells, then went into the forecastle for breakfast. The mate showed up again at 8 A.M. with his usual "Turn to, men." We spent the morning sweeping down the hold, rove off new spanker and fore boom tackle, and put some new hoops on the mizzen mast. After dinner we swept down the decks, coiled up all the loose running gear, and knocked off as it was Saturday afternoon. We spent the next hour or so scrubbing down the forecastle as, of course, sailors have to keep their quarters clean on their own time. Anchor watch was set again at 8 P.M. The wind was from the sou'east, a modest breeze.

Sunday broke clear and warm with a southerly wind that lasted all day. We spent our time washing and mending clothes, airing bedding, reading, smoking, and loafing. Toward evening a light fog set in. When the mate came forward to call out the anchor watch at 8 P.M., he said, "If it gets very thick get the foghorn out and if anything comes close, blow four or five short toots." We looked at him somewhat in wonder but he said nothing more, turned and walked aft. The foghorn is to be used only when a vessel is under way or it may be used to attract attention when a vessel is in distress.

The next morning, Monday, October 23, about 5 A.M., the mate called all hands to get under way. It was no false alarm this time, and going on

Looking forward at the fore, main, and mizzen topsails and lower sails. The spanker (left foreground) is reefed as indicated by the low position of the gaff and throat halliard block. Photo: J. S. McCullough

deck we found it blowing a fresh breeze from the nor'west. The gasoline donkey engine was started, the anchor hove short, and gaskets and stops were taken off the jibs and lower sails. The Old Man appeared on the poop deck, looked the situation over for a minute or so and sang out, "Set the mizzen." The mizzen throat and peak halliards were already led to the gypsyheads (one on each side of the forward house). The mate took his place by the mizzen sheet and gave the order, "Heave away together." Men at the gypsyheads took a few turns, blocks creaked, and the mizzen gaff started slowly up. When the luff of the sail was well stretched and the boom lifted clear of the saddle, the mate blew his whistle, a signal to stop heaving. "Belay the throat halliards," the mate ordered. A stopper was clapped on the halliards. "Come up the throat halliards," was the next order. A few turns around the belaying pin and the throat halliards were secure. "Heave away the peak," sang out the mate as he slacked the sheet a bit. When the leech of the sail was taut he blew his whistle again. The peak halliards were stopped off and belayed to the pin rail, the weather boom topping lift set, and that finished the job of setting the mizzensail. The mainsail was set next in very much the same manner, followed by the foresail. The anchor was then hove in and at the same time the forestaysail, jib, and flying jib were run up. "A man to the wheel," ordered the mate as the vessel filled away on the port tack and began to move slowly toward Swash Channel. It took about an hour to set sail, heave in the anchor, and get under way.

"We won't set the spanker yet for awhile," said the captain.

The mate gave the order, "Clear up the deck." The halliards were hauled back to their places and coiled down in the waterways clear for running, boom tackles hooked to the lee rail, lee topping lifts slacked off, and then we knocked off for breakfast. We passed around Scotland light vessel about 7:30 A.M. and the log was streamed. After breakfast we set the spanker, gybed the mizzen over, and the vessel ran off before the wind, wing and wing, on a course S ½ W (Var. 12 W) toward Barnegat light vessel, forty-one miles from Scotland. We set the main and fore topsails during the morning but soon clewed them up. The vessel, running light before the wind with a moderate swell, rolled too much to carry them. We sighted Barnegat light vessel with her black hull and white-lettered name off the starboard bow at 2 P.M. About that time the wind hauled around to the northeast and freshened up some. We were averaging 6.3 knots. We gybed the sails over on the port tack, shifted and set the fore and main topsails, and the schooner rolled along making eight or nine knots with all sail set but the mizzen and spanker topsails. The vessel had no outer jib bent.

During the first watch (8 P.M. to 12 M.) we ran through several rain squalls, the wind freshened, and the sky to windward looked threatening. The watch clewed up the fore and main topsails and tied them up. At eight bells (midnight), while both watches were on deck, we lowered the spanker and tied it up. The captain said the glass (barometer) was falling. During the middle watch (12 M. to 4 A.M.) the wind increased to a moderate gale with occasional rain squalls and kicked up a rough quartering sea. The vessel, having no ballast since it is not often carried in coastal schoon-

Looking aft at the main and mizzen topsails. The wind pennant can be seen at the truck of the spanker topmast. Photo: J. S. McCullough

ers, was high out of the water and dry on deck but she did roll. About daybreak the wind hauled to the eastward and moderated. The water was dark in color, indicating the vessel was in deep water, a hundred fathoms or more, so the course was changed to SSW (Var. 9.8 W). The mate took a sight for longitude (line of position) at 8 A.M. and according to his figures we were about seventy miles offshore.

The fore, main, and mizzen topsails were set at four bells (10 A.M.). It was blowing a moderate breeze and a heavy swell was running. The spanker was still tied up as the vessel was rolling too much to carry it safely and we were making about six knots without it. The flying jib, an old sail, began to go in some of the seams so we hauled it down, fixed it hurriedly, and set it again. By four bells in the afternoon the wind was light and baffling and we ran into a heavy rain squall. The topsails were clewed up and the lower sails gybed over on the starboard tack but a half hour later we wore ship. We tied up the topsails at eight bells (4 P.M.) in a drenching rain. The passing squall left us in a flat calm and the vessel rolled heavily in the big swells that were coming from the eastward. The booms and gaffs kept slamming and banging from side to side with such force it shook the vessel and it was not long before some of the sails began to go in the seams. Schooners are miserable things to be in when it is calm and a heavy swell is running.

At eight bells of the second dogwatch (8 P.M.) we hauled down the jibs and lowered the fore, main, and mizzen sails. The vessel fell off into the trough of the sea and everything that was not securely lashed down went adrift. A couple of empty meat casks we had on deck to catch rain water started playing tag with each other. Loose dunnage to be used for firewood ran races across the deck and a couple of buckets tried to batter themselves to pieces against the bulkhead every time the ship rolled. The pots and pans in the galley were having a hilarious time with the firewood and coal bucket. The vessel almost rolled the rails under and seemed about to snap the masts right out of her. A steamer passing close aboard signaled us with the Morse lamp, but no one in the vessel could send or receive the code and she soon disappeared into the night. Calm and heavy swells meant nothing to her as she plowed along toward her destination at ten or twelve knots.

About 10 P.M. we got a light breeze from the nor'west, a great relief after several hours without any wind. The watch below was called out and we set the main and mizzen sails, and the jib. The wind increased to a fresh breeze, the sky was clear, and at midnight we set the foresail. By the end of the middle watch (4 A.M.) it was blowing a gale. The vessel was hove to on the starboard tack, the wheel put hard down and in the beckets, but she would come up no closer than seven or eight points of the wind and then made a point or more leeway. The schooner lost part of her forefoot one time she grounded and it had never been replaced This interfered with her sailing qualities and handling. She would not tack except when loaded and conditions otherwise were favorable.

By daylight a heavy sea was running. The watch below was called out and the foresail was lowered and tied up. Extra stops were put on the spanker and more turns of the gasket taken around the flying jib. The wind shifted a few points to the north'ard, the vessel was kept on a SW course (Var. 8.0 W), and she was going along ten or eleven knots under jib, fore-staysail, main, and mizzen sails. At two bells in the afternoon Diamond Shoals light vessel was just visible on the starboard about five or six miles off, but we could not haul the *White* up for Frying Pan Shoals on account of the heavy seas, so the main and mizzen sails were lowered and tied up leaving the vessel under forestaysail and jib.

53

Metal steering wheel on the *White*. Just forward of this can be seen the binnacle, housing the compass, attached to the after trunk house. Photo: J. S. McCullough

Off Cape Hatteras the *Purnell T. White* runs before a northeast gale under bare poles. Looking aft from the forward house as the schooner rolls in heavy seas. Little water comes aboard as she has no cargo and rides high. Photo: J. S. McCullough

Heavy seas roll past the schooner's starboard rail as she runs south under bare poles off Cape Hatteras in October 1933. Photo: J. S. McCullough

We ran off to the SW all night under bare poles and the next morning we were out of the Gulf Stream. The wind and sea began to moderate as the vessel got under the lee of Cape Hatteras. At four bells (6 A.M.) it was daylight. The mizzen, main, and fore sails were set and the schooner put on a course W ½ S (Var. 5.0 W) to get into smoother water nearer the beach. We sailed about ten miles on this course then changed the course to WSW. At eight bells the flying jib was set and we discovered that the shell of one of the jib sheet blocks had been broken during the night. The jib was secured with a preventer sheet and I was left to replace the broken block. The preventer sheet had been made fast by the mate and in such a manner that it came adrift. The jib swung across the bowsprit with the roll of the vessel, struck me on the head and shoulder, and knocked me off the bowsprit. As I fell I grabbed hold of a stay and the toe of my shoe caught in the footrope which saved me from going overboard. The watch below heard the jib slapping and banging across the bowsprit, shaking the foremast, and threatening to tear itself to pieces. The men jumped out on deck, let the jib halliards go by the run, and manned the downhaul. The jib was soon under control, the broken block replaced, and the jib set again. I was very fortunate in not going overboard as there wasn't a life ring on the vessel, she would not heave to in the strong leading wind and following sea, and it is doubtful if the schooner's one boat, securely lashed to davits on the stern, could have been launched. I lost my cap overboard, the only one I had, got a bruised head, but considered myself lucky. And my estimation of the mate went down several points.

About four bells, forenoon watch, the wind veered to the northeast. The mainsail was gybed over and the vessel ran off before the wind, wing and wing, on the same course, WSW (Var. 4.0 W). We were making eight or nine knots and a coastal steamer had a hard time overhauling and passing us. We ran off before the wind, wing and wing, most of the day, sighting several steamers, the northbound steamers on the port side and the southbound ones on the starboard side.

We picked up Frying Pan Shoals light vessel off the starboard bow about 5:30 P.M. and had her abeam to windward a half mile off at 6 o'clock. The vessel was then hauled up on a course W ½ S (Var. 3.5 W) for Georgetown Bar, seventy-nine miles away. About dark the wind hauled a little more to the north'ard and freshened up. The flying jib was hauled down and tied up. On the first watch (8 P.M. until midnight), we made 44 miles by the patent log, our best run in one watch so far. The foresail was lowered and tied up at eight bells. We tried to take a sounding but the vessel was going too fast to get bottom. About 3 A.M. the lookout sighted Georgetown Light and a little later the sea buoy. All hands were called and the fore and main sails lowered, the jib and forestaysail hauled down, and a sounding taken. We were in seven fathoms of water. The anchors were cleared and we stood by to let go as soon as the vessel came up into the wind and lost headway. At 5:30 the starboard anchor was let go with seventy fathoms of cable out. The mizzensail was lowered and a couple stops put on all the sails, the deck cleared up of loose running gear, and both watches went

Looking aft along the clear deck of the schooner with lower sails wing-and-wing—that is, with the booms alternating from port to starboard so as to get full benefit of the strong, fair wind. Photo: J. S. McCullough

Jibboom, bowsprit, and two of the headsails. Photo: J. S. McCullough

After her run south along the coast, the *White* approaches Georgetown. Looking aft from fo'c'slehead along starboard side. Photo: J. S. McCullough

below with the exception of one man left to stand anchor watch. The sails were not securely tied up as we would use them to sail up Winyah Bay to Georgetown.

All hands were called out at 8 A.M. to put a new sheave in the mizzen peak halliard block and get some firewood up out of the hold for the cook.

Purnell T. White (left), at Georgetown, South Carolina, alongside the *Albert F. Paul*. Loading of the latter's cargo of lumber is nearing completion, November 1933. Photo: J. S. McCullough

Those jobs were finished in about an hour and we were told to stand by for the towboat and pilot. Captain Porter, the pilot, came off in his skiff and boarded us at about 11 o'clock. The wind was light and fair. The anchor was hove short and the spanker, mizzen, main, and fore sails were set, and we had dinner while we waited for the tide to turn flood. After dinner the anchor was hove in and at the same time the forestaysail and jib were run up. Next, the spanker topsail and flying jib were set as we headed for the entrance to the jetty and Winyah Bay. The towing hawser, mooring lines, and fenders were gotten up out of the hold where they had been stowed for the passage south. Inside the jetties the headsails were hauled down and the anchor let go about 2 P.M. The fore, main, and mizzen sails were lowered, the spanker topsail clewed up, and the spanker lowered. The spanker and topsail were tied up with a harbor furl as they would not be used anymore on the voyage. The rest of the sails had loose turns taken around them as they would be used again. This was Friday, October 27. We had three days and twenty-two hours from Scotland light vessel to the sea buoy off Georgetown Light. The most direct route by sea between these two points is 557 miles. We sailed about 577 miles for an average of 6.14 knots per hour. The best run in one watch (four hours) was 44 miles by patent log.

The captain was in no hurry to get to the dock as the four-masted schooner *Albert F. Paul* was alongside being loaded, and the dock, a small one, would accommodate only one vessel at a time.

We turned to the next morning at 8 A.M., hove short the anchor, washed down the decks, and stood by for the towboat. About noon a motor launch came alongside with the pilot. The port's only towboat, an old steam tug, the *W. H. Andrews* owned by the Atlantic Coast Lumber Company, was laid up so the motor launch was going to assist us to our berth. The launch was made fast on the port quarter and we waited for the tide to turn flood.

The mizzen, main, and fore sails were set and as soon as the tide had turned we hove in the anchor, setting the forestaysail, jib, and flying jib at the same time. With the aid of the tide and a light favorable wind the launch kept us in the channel and moving toward our destination. It is about 16 miles from the jetties up Winyah to the dock at Georgetown. When we were about a mile away from the dock we hauled down the head sails and the launch shifted over to the starboard quarter. As we approached the Tyson Lumber Company dock the fore, main, and mizzen sails were lowered. When we were opposite the dock the starboard anchor was let go and the vessel swung around in the stream and up alongside the *Albert F. Paul*. We made fast to her, tied up the sails, cleared up the deck of loose running gear, and knocked off. We were nine days from dock to dock. The average time for schooners is thirteen days.

John, Nick, and Andy didn't like the way things were turning out, for they wanted to get about two months out of the voyage and a halfway decent payday, if that was possible on thirty dollars a month. The way we were going the voyage wouldn't last more than a month.

It would be three or four days yet before the *Paul* was loaded and we could go alongside the loading berth. The Old Man gave us some money after supper, two dollars apiece, and we went off to see the town. We had ten dollars apiece wages due us for the time we were in the vessel and believed we were entitled, according to law, to draw half our wages. But the captain said he did not have that much money and, anyway, two dollars were enough to spend in one night in Georgetown.

The next day, Sunday, October 29, was spent visiting with the crew in the *Paul* and loafing around.

We turned to at 8 A.M. Monday morning. First, we unbent the jib and took it ashore to a large shed on the dock where we could repair it on a rainy day. Next, bos'n chairs were rigged on the fore, main, and mizzen topmasts and we started to scrape them down. Before we knocked off that evening the towing hawser was coiled down underneath the forecastlehead to keep it dry, and the decks were swept down.

We finished scraping and slushing down the topmasts the next day, and rigged the triangle on the foremast and began to scrape it down. The mainsail was unbent and taken to the shed ashore to be repaired at a later date. The decks were swept down and wood cut for the cook each evening after we knocked off about 4 P.M.

The *Albert F. Paul* finished loading Wednesday evening, November 1.

We turned to at 7 A.M. Thursday morning and hauled our vessel astern of the *Paul*. She breasted off and we warped in alongside of the dock to load. The longshoremen started to load the vessel at 8 A.M. They got twenty-four cents an hour under the NRA and worked eight hours a day. When I was in Georgetown several months ago, before the NRA was in effect, the longshoremen got from seven to nine and one-half cents an hour and worked ten hours a day.

The *Paul* tied up alongside of us to wait for a tug to come from Charleston and tow her to sea.

We finished scraping down the foremast that day and started on the mainmast. On Friday it rained, so we were all set to work sewing sail in the shed on the dock.

Saturday morning we finished scraping and slushing down the mainmast. In the afternoon we washed down the vessel fore and aft, made everything shipshape about the deck, and knocked off. The longshoremen worked half a day.

The crews of both schooners drew money and it wasn't long before the South Carolina corn liquor was flowing freely. At first the party was quite sociable; singing started, later to be followed by a fight and some knife play. No one was seriously injured but the *Paul*'s forecastle was pretty much of a wreck. By ten o'clock Sunday morning the money and liquor were all gone, most of the crew stretched out, and the rest of Sunday was quiet and peaceful.

Monday, we scraped down and slushed the spanker mast and started on the mizzen mast. The longshoremen did not work as there was no lumber on the dock. The lumber is brought in on trucks from little mills scattered back in the woods some ten or fifteen miles away.

Tuesday, we finished scraping and slushing down the masts. Wooden masts on schooners are scraped and slushed every two or three months and, if possible, the job is done in a southern port or in warm weather so that the grease will go on the mast smoothly and evenly. This helps to preserve the mast and also allows the mast hoops to slide more easily. When the masts are finished they are bright and shiny and look as if they had been well varnished. The masts finished, all hands were put to sewing sail; snake stitching, putting in new cloths or patches, and replacing chafed roping on the leeches.

Looking aft from the fore crosstrees of the *White*. The *Albert F. Paul*, at right, has completed her deck load and soon will be ready for sea. Photo: J. S. McCullough

On Wednesday, November 8, a towboat came from Charleston and towed the *Paul* to sea. We were still sewing sail.

Thursday was the first day of the week the longshoremen worked, as the roads were bad and the trucks could not get the lumber in from the mills. We brought the jib aboard, bent it, and took the foresail ashore to repair.

The longshoremen worked a few hours on Friday and we sewed sail all day. We finished the mainsail, brought it aboard, and bent it.

Saturday, November 11, we sewed sail for a while in the morning. Then we came aboard, cleaned up the decks, washed down fore and aft, replenished the cook's firewood, and knocked off for the day at noon.

Sunday was a quiet day spent washing clothes and loafing. No one had any money.

Monday, we replaced broken ratlines and battens on the mizzen and spanker shrouds and oiled the decks with pine oil. The longshoremen did not work. About dark a heavy squall from the sou'west hit us and we were called to put extra mooring on the dock. There was heavy rain with the squall and we were soaked to the skin.

Tuesday, we painted the inside of the bulwarks white and the waterways green. This job had to be done before the deck load was put aboard.

Wednesday, we finished painting the bulwarks and waterways and started repairing ratlines and battens on the fore and main shrouds. That afternoon we took aboard about half a ton of coal for the cabin stove and cut more wood for the cook.

We brought the foresail aboard on Thursday and bent it, then painted the anchors and bobstay chains, and washed the paintwork on the poop deck. The longshoremen finished loading the after hatch and we battened it down. A half ton of coal was delivered alongside while we were eating supper so we had to turn to and take it aboard.

The main and fore hatches were loaded Friday morning and we battened them down after we cut a good supply of firewood on the dock, brought it aboard, and stowed it in the fore hatch. The towing hawser was broken out and coiled down on the forecastlehead. Three hundred pounds of ice were delivered alongside in the afternoon and taken aboard and stowed in the ice chest. The longshoremen finished loading all cargo about 4 P.M. The deck load extended from the after part of the fore hatch to the break of the poop and to the height of the bulwarks. We had aboard 535,000 feet of green hard pine, boards, planks, and square timber. The vessel drew sixteen feet nine inches of water (fresh) aft.

Saturday morning, November 18, we turned out at 8 A.M. to get the vessel ready for sea. Chain deckload lashings were brought up from the forward lazarette, put in place, and set up with turnbuckles. The spanker was loosed, reefed and tied up again. The skipper did not believe in starting on a voyage north of Hatteras in the wintertime with a full spanker. The port hawse and chain pipes were plugged and cemented. The fore, main, mizzen, and spanker sheets were rove off. They had been made up and stowed below for protection for the duration of our stay in port. We built a temporary rail along each side of the deck load. The vessel was now in good shape to go to sea and we expected the towboat from Charleston in the morning.

Purnell T. White alongside lumber wharf at Georgetown, South Carolina, loaded and ready to sail for New York. Photo: J. S. McCullough

Chapter 6

THE weather broke clear and warm the next day with a light easterly wind. Captain Porter, the pilot, came aboard about 8:30 and we singled up the mooring lines. An hour later the towboat *Hinton* came steaming up the river to tow us to sea. We were all glad to get away from the warm days and nights and mosquitoes of Georgetown. We passed the towing hawser to the tug and started to let go the remaining mooring lines when we discovered that Chubby, the cat, was not on board. The vessel was then five or six feet away from the dock but Jimmy, the cook, jumped ashore and started calling and searching for Chubby among the lumber piles. Chubby suddenly appeared from under a pile of lumber and headed toward the schooner, but a stray dog that happened to be on the dock saw Chubby and took after her. In the rush and excitement Chubby fell overboard but was rescued by Jimmy, brought aboard, and put to dry behind the galley stove. The mooring lines were cast off and hauled aboard and we were on our way down the river.

After the vessel was out in the bay the towboat made fast on the starboard quarter where she stayed until we got down to the jetties. Then she took the hawser and towed us out through the jetties to the bar where we anchored about 1:30 P.M. The wind was light and from the east, a head wind. The towboat let go the hawser and with three blasts of her whistle as a parting salute she headed off toward Charleston. A skiff came alongside to get the pilot. Wishing the Old Man "a fair wind and fast passage," the pilot boarded his skiff and headed back for Georgetown. We spent the afternoon washing clothes and whistling for a wind but I guess we were somewhat out of tune as 8 P.M. came around and the high fly, or wind sock, at the spanker topmast truck showed no sign of a breeze. We turned in early, except the man whose turn it was to stand anchor watch.

About 11:30 P.M. a light breeze sprang up from the SW and it was "all hands to get under way." The anchor was hove in and at the same time the forestaysail, jib, and flying jib were set, followed by the foresail, main-sail, mizzen, and reefed spanker. The vessel filled away on the starboard tack about 1 A.M., November 20. The fore, main, and mizzen topsails were set. The spanker topsail could not be set as the spanker was reefed. It took an hour and a half to heave in the anchor and set sail but our work wasn't over as the anchor came in with a turn in the cable and would not stow properly. After numerous attempts we got a messenger over the fluke of the anchor and hove it around so that it would go into the hawse pipe. The

Looking forward on the starboard side, bound north with her hold and deck stacked with lumber, November 1933. Photo: J. S. McCullough

Looking forward on the port side from the quarterdeck. Photo: J. S. McCullough

Under two headsails, a full mizzen, and reefed foresail, mainsail, and spanker, the *Purnell T. White* sails steadily northward. Photo: J. S. McCullough

halliards and other running gear were coiled clear for running, or hung on belaying pins, and at 2 A.M. the mate called out, "Watch below, go below."

The light southwest wind lasted about three hours then shifted around to the north northwest and freshened up. The topsails were clewed and the lower sails gybed over on the port tack. The main topsail was shifted and set but the fore and mizzen topsails were left hanging in the clew lines. We had a very red sunrise, the wind hauled around a little more to the nor'ward, the sheets were trimmed in "by the wind," and the fore and mizzen topsails were shifted and set. The starboard hawse and chain pipes were plugged and cemented. The watch on deck spent the day scraping and varnishing the bitts and brightwork on the corners of the deckhouses. About noon the wind died out and the topsails were clewed up. After supper the towing hawser was coiled down in the lazarette. The sun set clear and red which caused John to quote the sailor's adage, "When the sun goes down clear as a bell, easterly winds sure as hell." We looked for Frying Pan light vessel ahead or a little on the port bow but it wasn't until after dark that we picked up the light blinking a point or so off the port bow. During the first watch (8 P.M. to midnight) a light breeze sprang up from the east, but it was hardly enough to keep the sails full and steerageway on the vessel. During the night the wind remained light and variable and we did not gain much on the lightship. She bore E two or three miles off just before daylight.

About 9 A.M. the Savannah Line steamer *City of Chattanooga* passed astern of us close aboard. The rails were lined with passengers and crew. A sailing vessel under way, even an old schooner, was getting to be an unusual sight those days. About 9:30 we got a light breeze from the SSE. The booms were hauled over on the starboard tack, the topsails shifted and set, and by 10:30 we had the light vessel abeam. The watch on deck, when not working the ship, spent their time during the day painting the cap rails. The wind veered to SW about 5 P.M. We clewed up the topsails and tried to wear ship but she would not go around. A strong current was carrying her to the eastward and the wind was not strong enough to overcome the current. The sun set red behind a heavy cloud bank and the breeze freshened up. The sails were gybed over on the port tack and when the watch was changed at 8 P.M. the spanker was lowered and tied up as the sky to windward looked threatening and the wind was increasing. By midnight, November 22, it was blowing a strong breeze. The mizzen topsail, the only one set, was clewed up and made fast. The vessel was rolling along almost before the wind in a rough sea, making about eight knots. The course toward Diamond Shoals light vessel was about NE and the wind was strong and steady from the SW, so during the middle watch (midnight to 4 A.M.) we lowered the foresail and hauled down the flying jib because they would not draw. The mainsail was gybed over and we ran directly before the wind, wing and wing.

By 6 A.M. the wind had gone around to the west so we set the foresail and gybed the mainsail over on the port tack. After breakfast the watch on deck repaired the spanker which had been damaged when we last lowered it. The wind kept increasing and the sea getting rougher. We went around

Diamond Shoals light vessel at noon making about 10 knots and shipping seas over both rails. After we got about a mile to the eastward of the light vessel we hauled up on a north course. Seas and spray were coming aboard now and the watch on deck could do no work. They stood by on the cabin trunk trying to keep dry and be ready for any emergency that might arise.

Chubby, the cat, had been marooned in the cabin but the cabin was cold and damp and perhaps there wasn't much for a cat to eat there. Anyway, she decided to go forward to the galley where it was warm and her friend Jimmy, the cook, would be sure to give her something to eat. She succeeded in getting safely across the deck load with nothing more than wet feet, and almost reached the galley door, when a sea came over the starboard rail and half filled the deck. Chubby was washed across the deck and back again but luckily Jimmy saw her and went to the rescue. Half drowned, the cat was put to dry in the woodbox back of the galley stove.

Early in the afternoon an Eastern Steamship Company steamer, bound south, passed to windward, and the Morgan Line steamer *El Coston*, bound north, overhauled and passed us close aboard without much difficulty. Wind and sea moderated rapidly after we got around Hatteras and we loosened and set the flying jib. Late in the afternoon we ran out of the Gulf Stream and into green water and soon we saw and heard Wimble Shoals buoy whistling away off the weather bow. The weather until then had been warm but it became damp and chilly and we realized that we were going north in the wintertime.

We had Bodie Island light abeam at 8 P.M. The sky was overcast, the sea smooth, and there was very little wind. We could have been carrying the spanker and topsails for several hours but the Old Man wasn't much of a driver and he did not have much faith in the mate's ability as a sailor. Any fool can set sail but you have to be a sailor to take it in in a gale of wind. We, forward, hated to be drifting along under short sail with a fair wind blowing.

Thursday, November 23. During the night we had a light westerly wind, the sky was cloudy, and it was quite cold. We sighted lots of steamers inshore but none passed close to us. About 4 bells of the morning watch a thick fog set in. The foghorn (a large box containing a reed horn with bellows attached and worked by a handle on the outside of the box) was placed up on the forecastlehead and put in operation, two blasts at more or less regular intervals, the signal for a sailing vessel under way on the port tack. Visibility improved at about 8 bells and the signal was discontinued.

During the morning we set the spanker and the mizzen topsail. The wind hauled around to NW and the sheets were trimmed in "by the wind." If the spanker and topsails had been set yesterday when we had a fair wind we might have been almost to the latitude of Cape Henry. About noon the wind hauled more to the north'ard and freshened up. At 2 P.M. we took in the mizzen topsail and flying jib. An hour later all hands were called to reef the fore and main sails. The wind had increased to a fresh gale and kicked up a rough sea which was breaking over the weather bow. The vessel was pitching and rolling some and the deck load had started to work loose. As soon as we had the sails reefed and set we turned to on the deck load

Looking aft along the starboard side. The chains that secure the deck load can be clearly seen. The spanker has been furled with fore, main, and mizzen sails full. Photo: J. S. McCullough

As viewed from the top of the forward house over the port rail, the *White*, urged on by a strong wind, pushes the seas aside. Photo: J. S. McCullough

lashings and set them up. The vessel was now hove to on the port tack heading about northeast with the wheel hard down and in the beckets.

During the night the wind moderated and by 6 A.M. of the 24th it was a flat calm. The vessel lay in the trough of the sea, the sails slamming and banging across the deck as she rolled in the big swells. About 10 A.M. the mate took a sight and estimated our position as thirty miles northeast of Diamond Shoals light vessel. A sounding showed twenty-four fathoms of water. We had been set southeastward about twenty-five miles in the last fifteen or twenty hours.

The Dollar Line steamer *President Wilson* passed us close aboard during the morning, southward bound. We spent the day at various jobs such as making a new main topping lift from an old cargo runner we found on the dock, painting the windlass, and tightening reef points. The jaw on the mizzen boom began to work loose and upon examining the boom closely it was found to be affected with dry rot. It looked sound from the outside but the inside was rotten. We fished it with pieces of 2″ x 4″, wire, and rope lashings tightened with wedges. It was calm all day, a regular Paddy's hurricane, and the sea was as smooth as glass except for the heave of the swells. During the first watch (8 P.M. to 12 M.) we gybed the sails over several times trying to catch the cat's-paws that came from various quarters, but it was not until 2 A.M. that we got a gentle breeze from the NNW and filled away on the port tack after about 22 hours of calm. The watch on deck shook the reefs out of the fore and main sails, set the flying jib, and streamed the log.

About 6 A.M. the wind hauled around to the NE. We wore ship, set the fore, main, and mizzen topsails and headed up on a course N by W (Var. 7 W). At noon, according to the mate's calculations, Cape Henry bore WNW forty-seven miles, and a sounding showed sixteen fathoms of water. The course was changed to N to fetch Winterquarter light vessel. We did not do much work on deck, just stood our wheel watches and worked the ship. The latter part of the day the wind went around a little more to the eastward but remained light.

Sunday, November 26. We clewed up the topsails during the middle watch (12 M. to 4 A.M.) and gybed over on the port tack. The wind remained light and variable and we did not set the topsails again. Day broke with an overcast sky, hazy horizon, and very little wind. During the forenoon a dense fog set in and the foghorn was broken out and put in operation. The sky overhead looked threatening and there was a heavy swell running, so about 10 A.M. we tied up the topsails and waited for some change in the weather. Just before noon the fog lifted but the sky remained overcast. During the afternoon the flying jib was hauled down and tied up, then the foresail was lowered and secured with a peak stop. Fog set in again late in the afternoon. We heard a steamer whistling off to windward but she did not pass close to us.

During the dogwatch a light breeze set in from the SW and the visibility improved. The sky cleared and the moon showed brightly for a little while. The wind shifted suddenly around to the WNW; then came a flash of lightning and thunder. A heavy, dark cloud bank came up rapidly from the NW. All hands were called and about that time the wind hit us, a cold hard squall followed by a little rain. The main and mizzen halliards were let go and the sails hauled down and secured as quickly as possible. After the first squall we had a short period of calm, then the wind came again from the WNW much colder and with gale force. We reefed the mizzen, main, and fore sails and set them. The vessel was going "by the wind" heading about N by W and taking plenty of water over the weather bow.

The men who had the watch below were waiting for the mate to order, "Watch below, go below," for an hour or so of rest before they would be called to relieve the watch on deck at midnight. We shipped an extra heavy sea which started the deck load to work loose and washed some planks overboard. It was another "all hands" job to set up the lashings and secure the deck load. The mate stood by in the weather main rigging to give warning to hold fast or stand clear when a heavy sea was about to break aboard. By midnight everything was as secure as we could make it. One watch went below and the watch on deck went aft to the poop deck, the driest part of the vessel. Even the poop deck was awash at times. The mate and sailor not at the wheel could jump up on the wheel box or cabin trunk and keep dry but the man at the wheel had to stay and take it. We stood only one hour wheel watch at a time as it was quite cold.

When we were relieved to go below at 4 A.M., we had to watch our chance to go forward without being swept off our feet and perhaps overboard. We found the forecastle awash with about a foot of water on deck. Everything that had not been securely stowed had gone adrift. Most of it was on deck rolling from side to side in the water. The deck head (top of the forward house) had been badly started and every time the vessel took a sea over the forecastlehead it raced aft, hit the deckhouse with force, and came gushing into the forecastle in torrents. The bogie funnel (smokestack for the little stove in the forecastle) had been washed away and water poured through the poorly plugged hole. Water spurted in around the door and port every time a sea hit them. We tried to bail out the forecastle but it was useless. There wasn't much comfort in going to bed as the bunks were as wet or wetter, if possible, than we were. The only part of the forecastle that was anywhere near dry was the after end of the top inboard bunk, and there we piled our shore-going clothes to protect them as best we could. We did have dry matches and tobacco, so we sat and smoked and waited to see if the cook would come forward at the usual time, about 4:30, to make coffee for the watch. He did, but the minutes waited seemed like hours, longer than the hour spent at the wheel. With much mumbling and cursing he got a fire started, but it was difficult to keep the pot on the stove and the coffee in the pot. Eventually, the coffee was boiled and it was a welcome sound when he pounded on the bulkhead and shouted, "Come and get it," a pot of coffee and a pan of hard biscuits.

At breakfast time the cook reported Chubby missing. A search started immediately but it was quite some time before the little grey kitten was found, away under the forecastlehead crouched on the bowsprit, wet, cold, crying, and badly scared. She was taken into the forecastle and stowed snugly away in the dry bunk with the shore-going gear.

The gale held on all morning. The schooner seemed to be weathering it all right and making some headway, for at noon we had Winterquarter light vessel abeam to leeward. As we got in closer to the beach the sea moderated considerably. We rigged a funnel for the bogie but could not get a fire started because of the back draft from the foresail. Toward evening the wind moderated and the sky cleared but it remained quite cold. At 9:30 P.M. we had Fenwick Shoals buoy abeam. The wind slowly hauled to the westward and moderated as a fresh breeze so we shook the reefs out of the main and mizzen sails and the vessel was put on a course NE by N for Five Fathom Bank light vessel. The wind shifted on around to SW, the sheets were slacked off, and shortly before midnight we sighted Five Fathom Bank light vessel right ahead.

At 1 A.M., Tuesday, November 28, we had the light vessel abeam close aboard. The wind hauled around to the west'ard and freshened up enough to drive the vessel along at eight or nine knots under short sail. Just before dawn we saw the loom of Atlantic City lights in the western sky. The vessel steered quite badly with the spanker set and not much head sail. The foresail was still reefed and the flying jib tied up. Shortly after daybreak we took in the spanker and the vessel steered much better. We passed to leeward of Brigantine Shoals buoy about 6 A.M. and the course was changed to NE by N (Var. 10 W) for Barnegat light vessel.

After breakfast, with both watches on deck, we set the main topsail, flying jib, shook the reef out of the foresail, and set the main and mizzen topsails. When that job was finished, John said ,"If we kin hold this wind we might be home for Thanksgiving yet, but I don't know what good that would do." At 10 A.M. we set the spanker and an hour later we had Barnegat light vessel abeam. The course was changed to N for Scotland light vessel forty-one miles away, and about the same time the wind hauled to WNW. The sheets were trimmed in flat and the steering order was "full and by." During the afternoon the wind moderated to a light breeze and when we passed Shrewsbury Rock buoy about 8 P.M., we were not making much more than steerageway and with a favorable tide. The plugs were knocked out of the starboard hawse and chain pipes as it looked as if we would soon have to anchor.

At midnight the wind hauled around to the north, a light breeze, and we clewed up the topsails, wore ship, and stood in toward the beach. A sounding at 2 A.M. showed fifteen fathoms of water. At 2:30 we got twelve fathoms and at 3:00 we were in ten fathoms. The watch below was called out and we hauled down the head sails, brought the vessel up into the wind, and about 3:30 let go the starboard anchor with thirty-five fathoms of chain out.

That was the end of our sea passage. Navesink Light bore W½N two and one-half miles off, and Scotland light vessel bore N⅓E about three miles off. We lowered the sails and left them hanging in the lifts as there was very little wind. The plugs were knocked out of the port hawse and chain pipes, anchor watch was set, and the watch below went below about 4 A.M.

The mate called all hands at 5 A.M. to get under way but there was no wind, so we just sat around drinking coffee and cursing him. Many were the threats as to what would be done to him when he went ashore. The port watch had the forenoon watch on deck, and the mate turned them to at eight bells to do a lot of unnecessary work about the deck. About 11 A.M. a light breeze sprang up from the east'ard and the watch below was called out to get under way. The anchor was hove short and the mizzen, main, and fore sails set. The forestaysail and jib were run up and trimmed to windward to box the vessel off on the starboard tack, and at the same time the anchor was hove in. When she filled away and was headed toward Swash Channel the flying jib and spanker were set, followed by the fore, main, and mizzen topsails. We passed Scotland light vessel close aboard about 1 P.M. The towing hawser was broken out and coiled down on the forecastlehead to be ready for the towboat which we expected to see any moment coming down the bay to meet us.

At 2 P.M. the watch below was called out again to take in sail. It was almost calm and the Old Man had given up hope for a tow that day as the tide had been running flood for over two hours. Our ship and cargo were not important enough to tow in against an ebb tide. We lowered the spanker and tied it up for the last time. The topsails were clewed up and harbor furled for they would not be used again. The mizzensail was winged out and we ran before the light southeast wind until it died out completely about 3 P.M. The foresail and mainsail were lowered and the head sails hauled down. When the vessel had lost all way, the starboard anchor was let go. We were well inside of Sandy Hook. The mizzensail was lowered and all the sails were tied up. We were all pretty much in bad humour as we had hoped to get to the dock and be paid off in time to spend the holiday ashore, although we were probably better off anchored safely off Sandy Hook. But as has been said before, one might as well be a thousand miles at sea as anchored off Sandy Hook.

On Thanksgiving Day, November 30, the wind was fresh from the northwest and a head wind for sailing into the upper bay. We were not called to do any work except stand anchor watch.

Friday morning we turned to, both watches, and let go the deck load lashings, broke out the mooring lines, sewed some sail, and repaired rigging until 4 P.M. Then we knocked off for the day.

The mate called all hands at 5 the next morning. I don't know why for we sat around until after breakfast, then rigged the deck pump and washed down the decks that were not covered with deck load. Then we knocked off. About 3 P.M. we sighted a towboat coming down the bay with a three-masted schooner in tow. The schooner had her lower sails set. Off Sandy Hook the tug let go the vessel's hawser, the topsails were sheeted home, and she filled away on the starboard tack bound south. As she crossed our bow she ran her ensign up to the mizzen truck and dipped in salute. The tug *John B. Caddell* came alongside to take our towline and told us that the three-master was the *Frank A. Morey.*

We passed the hawser to the tug, hove in the anchor, set the mainsail and forestaysail, and were on our way. Going through the Narrows a Coast Guard boat hailed us and came alongside and put a couple men on board to look at the ship's papers. Apparently they were found to be in order for they did not detain us. Approaching the anchorage we lowered the mainsail and hauled down the forestaysail and gave them a harbor furl. On Red Hook flats the towboat brought the schooner up into the wind and cast off the hawser. We let go the starboard anchor, cleared up the deck, and knocked

Looking aft from the jibboom as the *White* was anchored off Sandy Hook, New Jersey, Thanksgiving Day 1933, awaiting a tug to tow her to an anchorage off Red Hook, Brooklyn, New York. Photo: J. S. McCullough

off about 7 P.M. Anchored on the flats were five steamers, several barges, but only one sailing vessel besides ourselves. She was the full-rigged ship *Tusitala.*

When we went into the forecastle John said, "I suppose all the schooner stiffs ashore are lined up on South Street waiting for this old raft to drift in."

The skipper sent word forward that anyone who wanted to go ashore could have five dollars. But we all were tired and glad of a chance to turn in for a good night's sleep unbroken by an anchor watch or perhaps a call for all hands. We trimmed and lit the anchor lights and ran them up. Then all hands turned in leaving the vessel to take care of herself.

At 9 A.M. Sunday, December 3, the mate turned us to on a leaking water tank to make repairs. We finished the job about 1 P.M. A bumboat came alongside during the afternoon and we bought some newspapers.

The next morning at 8 the mate called us out to do some odd jobs about the deck—anything to keep us happy and busy. The boat flag was run up after breakfast and the Old Man went ashore about 10 A.M. He came back aboard about 4 P.M., called us down to the cabin, and paid us off. We had one month and sixteen days pay coming, which amounted to forty-six dollars less draws and slops. By the time we were paid off and had our supper it was dark, so the skipper told us we could stay aboard until morning. The vessel was not going to dock until the schooner *Albert F. Paul* finished discharging and got away from the berth. The mate and cook were all the men needed to moor the ship. Then, as was the custom in schooners, the mate would be paid off and the cook would stay by the vessel as shipkeeper and cook for the captain. He would receive no wages until the schooner got another charter and shipped a crew. He did have room and board and not much work to do.

That night about 8 a U. S. Customs boat came alongside and three men boarded us. They searched the vessel and looked at the ship's papers. This was quite common during Prohibition.

On Tuesday, December 5, we were up bright and early without the mate calling us. We bathed, shaved, packed our gear, and dressed in our shore-going clothes. Jimmy the cook gave us some coffee. Of course, we could not expect anything to eat as we had been paid off. We ran up the boat flag and soon a junk-boat came alongside. After some bargaining the boatmen agreed to put us ashore in Erie Basin for a dollar apiece, a day's pay for a three-quarter mile boat ride.

We had eight days, fourteen hours and thirty minutes from the George-town sea buoy to an anchorage off Scotland light vessel, the end of the sea passage. We sailed approximately 605 nautical miles at an average speed of 2.9 knots. The best day's run, noon November 21 to noon November 22, was 145 miles, an average speed of 6 knots. For the complete voyage, New York to Georgetown and back (sea passage), we sailed approximately 1,182 miles in twelve days, twelve hours and thirty minutes at an average speed of 3.9 knots. (This is not to be taken as a record or an average speed of a sailing vessel.)

People sometimes ask me what sailors do at sea. This is a fairly accurate and detailed account of life aboard a sailing vessel, an American coasting schooner, during the early 1930's.

80

Chapter 7

LITTLE did seaman McCullough realize that he was making the next to last voyage of the *Purnell T. White*. On the following trip north from Georgetown, with a cargo of lumber from the mill of Rankin and Tyson, the schooner was to encounter weather beyond her endurance. This was to end her days under sail.

With a full hold and her deck cargo securely chained against heavy seas, the *White* left Georgetown on January 27, 1934, bound for New York. Captain Charles Nicklas was in command and he had no reason to believe this passage would be any more difficult than the numerous other trips he had made in heavily laden schooners along the coast in the dead of winter. His ship was well found and had been hauled out, caulked, and painted the previous June. The sails and gear were in good condition and within several weeks or less the vessel could possibly be at her destination. Still, one could never count on predicting a quick winter northbound passage in a coasting schooner. There was always the expectancy of gales from the northeast or northwest to lash coastal shipping and a sailing ship would do well to hold her own against these conditions.

No doubt the *Purnell T. White* did meet heavy weather as she steered northward for she was only 200 miles east of Cape Fear, North Carolina, on February 7. She had made little progress. On that date, while flying distress signals, she was sighted by the steamer *Maiden Creek* bound for England. Her battle with winter gales was evidenced in the loss of her sails. Here was a task for the Coast Guard so the steamer relayed a message to the Norfolk base for assistance to be sent to the schooner. The nearest cutter on patrol was the *Mendota* which requested the steamer to stand by the disabled schooner until aid reached her.

The temperature was below freezing and a dense vapor rising from the warmer waters reduced visibility to a few hundred yards. A northerly gale was blowing and it was snowing heavily. Meanwhile, a smaller Coast Guard patrol boat, the *Tiger*, which was closer to the *White*, was ordered to proceed to the schooner. The radio operator of the *Maiden Creek* was asked to transmit signals so that both Coast Guard vessels could take bearings and steer directly to the scene. Within seven hours the *Tiger* was alongside the *White* and the *Maiden Creek* resumed her passage. The *Mendota* arrived an hour and a half later and took over from the smaller *Tiger* which carried on her patrol duty.

The steamship *Maiden Creek* encountered the *Purnell T. White* in distress on February 7, 1934, and relayed a message to the Coast Guard for assistance to be sent to the schooner. Photo: U. S. Coast Guard, The Mariners Museum

A line was shot to the *White* by the *Mendota* and by this the crew of the schooner pulled over a twelve-inch hawser to be used to tow her to safety. Shortly after midnight the cutter got under way slowly for the haven of the Virginia capes. The *White*'s pumps were inoperative and she was leaking. Part of her deck load had been carried away but the lumber in the hold kept the schooner afloat.

Mendota, the 250-foot Coast Guard cutter that attempted to tow the *Purnell T. White* to safety when the schooner was overwhelmed by heavy weather. Photo: E. P. Griffith, The Mariners Museum

Favorable progress was made as the weather moderated but that evening a northeaster developed and the cutter had to reduce speed. The *Mendota* tried to ride out the storm with just sufficient headway to maintain steerage and to keep the *White*'s bow into the seas. But the effect of the heavy winds on both vessels brought them dangerously close to the shoals off False Cape, Virginia, south of Cape Henry.

As daylight of the 9th approached, the wind shifted to the north and northwest and blew a fresh gale. Thick vapor and a blinding blizzard added to the difficulties. The *Mendota* created an oil slick astern to enable the schooner to ride more easily. At 10:50 A.M. signal flags indicating, "I am waterlogged and in danger of sinking," were observed on the *White*. The schooner seemed to roll erratically through the snow and vapor, heavier to starboard than to port.

That evening flares were sent up from the listing *White* which implied that her crew wished to be taken off. Because of the high seas and wind, rescue attempts with a small boat were doubtful. So the cutter's commander decided to try to bring his ship alongside the schooner to effect a rescue. Heaving lines, a life raft, life preservers, shoulder line-throwing gun, and other equipment were readied on the cutter's deck. Jacob's ladders were hung on each side of her bow. The towing hawser was cast off the *Mendota* and she made a sweep around through the spume and snow to approach the *White*'s stern. A line was shot to her and a life raft was passed over attached to a three-inch rope. When the raft was pulled back to the cutter, one seaman, L. C. Spencer, was aboard. The raft was pulled back to the schooner and this time it was returned to the cutter with seaman John Olsen and the negro cook Jim Lee. As they reached the side of the *Mendota*, members of her crew clung to ladders to assist them to safety but a sea swept the raft away and the men were washed overboard. Lifelines were thrown to the two men but, exhausted and numb from the cold, they were unable to grasp the lines and disappeared in the darkness.

Four men were still on the *White* which was almost on her beam ends and being raked by the seas. The *Mendota*'s bow was nudged against the schooner's stern. Lifelines were hurled to the derelict's deck and two sailors, Ragnor Lind and Nick Ivison, grabbed hold and were lifted to the cutter's deck. The mate, John Rider, reached for a lifeline but slipped and was lost in the sea. Captain Nicklas remained on his ship. He seized a line, secured it around his waist, and jumped into the sea. The line fouled on the schooner's wreckage and the 74-year old skipper was carried under the vessel and lost.

On August 10, 1927, a short item in the shipping news of the *Baltimore Sun* began:

> Captain Charles Nicklas of Baltimore, having resigned command of the schooner *Purnell T. White*, has recorded 48 years of sea life. He has purchased a farm near Westminster (Maryland) and has already started as a breeder of chickens . . .

Captain Nicklas had long been in sail. He was born in Scandinavia and came to the United States as a young man of 19 to search for gold. Apparently, he found none of the glittering metal so took to the sea since he had some experience as a sailor. For a while he sailed in the colorful "coffee fleet," the sailing vessels which plied between Baltimore and Rio de Janeiro. Then he engaged in the coasting trade until the purchase of his farm.

Perhaps the lure of the sea was too strong for him to remain landbound as he did find his way back to the quarterdeck of the *White* which he had commanded previously. One who sailed with Captain Nicklas described him as "addicted to long stretches of silence, not speaking more than a few words at a time." "If the Old Man had ever spoken more than six words continuously, barring orders," one of his crew once said, "his men never suspected it."

Captain Nicklas considered Georgetown, South Carolina, his second home since he called there so regularly and there he described to his friends his Westminster farm and his flower garden, poultry yard, flourishing orchards, and various interests that centered about the place which he could visit only at intervals between voyages. But he never mentioned retirement.

The dismasted wreck of the *White* arrives at Berkley, Virginia, assisted by the tug *Carl D. Colonna,* on February 15, 1934. Photo: Charles Borjes

Searchlights swept the turbulent seas for the lost men, but in vain. The *Mendota,* fearing that her propeller would become snarled in the trailing rigging of the schooner, pushed the hulk to windward and then backed away. Soon the *Purnell T. White* was lost to sight. After further search for survivors, the cutter steamed on to Norfolk with the three rescued men who were suffering from exposure to the cold. The *White* was left wallowing in the blackness of the night, a solid bulk of timbers and a menace to navigation.

The next day the cutter *Ponchartrain* was dispatched to search for the derelict, found her, and towed her into Chesapeake Bay to Lynnhaven Roads, behind Cape Henry. There the Norfolk tug *Carl D. Colonna* took her over to bring her to Colonna's shipyard at Berkley, Virginia.

85

During her struggle at sea the *White* was dismasted as she lay on her beam ends. Free of these spars, she righted herself. As she lay at Colonna's, water covered her main deck and starboard bulwark, her spanker mast and boom lay across the gaping hole that was once her after cabin. The superstructure of this cabin had been swept away and the former living quarters were littered with wreckage. Her poop and fo'c'slehead were free of water. Another fallen mast lay athwartship of her main deck tangled with twisted shrouds. Fragments of her headsails were draped over her bow. Her metal steering wheel had been shattered by the falling spanker mast or spanker

The hulk is pumped out and the tangled rigging cleared up at Berkley. Photo: Vollmer

boom. The wheelbox had been washed away, exposing the gears and shafts of her steering equipment. The falling spars had also torn away her taffrail, stern davits, and yawl boat.

At Colonna's most of the wreckage was cleared away and the hold pumped free of water. Except for a hole on her port quarter, where she was buffeted by the *Mendota* in the surging seas, her hull was intact. But this was brought above water as the pumps released her of her liquid burden.

Her owner, R. B. White, came down to Norfolk to view the wreck. He soon dismissed any hopes he may have had of rebuilding and rerigging his ship. But the lumber cargo in her hold had to be discharged, so he ordered the hulk to be towed to Baltimore where a decision would be made as to the fate of the *Purnell T. White*.

R. B. White, managing owner of the schooner, examines the battered steering gear.
Photo: Vollmer

On March 23, at the end of a towline behind the tug *Fannie May*, the *White* arrived at Baltimore and was tied up at Shryock's lumber wharf. A harbor that she had entered numerous times as a sturdy, seagoing ship now looked upon a completely battered wreck. A light early spring snow dusted her debris-strewn decks and cabins. Her long jibboom, dolphin striker and tangled rigging under her bows had been removed at Berkley. Only a stumpy bowsprit carried forward her sheer which, even after the strenuous battle with the heavy seas, she still retained. Still projecting over her stern was her spanker boom.

Upon arrival in Baltimore on March 23, 1934, the *Purnell T. White* was tied up at Shryock's lumber wharf. The eagle figurehead can be seen. Photo: Author

The galley in the forward deckhouse was made habitable for a watchman to ward off curious sightseers who might have wanted to prowl about the derelict. Yet, strangely enough, even though here was a living story of a ship's tremendous struggle with a winter's gale, the onlookers were few. Moored in a rather inaccessible part of the waterfront the schooner was inconvenient to reach. The watchman had little to do except tend the pumps and mooring lines.

As the lumber was removed from her hold and stacked on the adjacent dock, the hull slowly rose out of the water. In April she was towed to the McGrath Company pier, off Boston Street, where the discharging was completed. There she lay for a brief period as her owner decided what to do with the vessel. That decision was arrived at without much delay. It would be too costly to repair and rerig the otherwise seaworthy hull. The future for large sailing ships looked rather grim by the early 1930's, although this particular schooner had kept busy prior to that time.

These massive bows had cleaved numerous stormy seas in the schooner's 16 years of active sailing. Photo: Author

The forward starboard side of the schooner. Photo: **Author**

The *White*'s after starboard side. Photo: **Author**

Looking forward along the length of the schooner's deck showing the havoc wrought by the storm. Photo: Author

Looking forward from the starboard quarterdeck. In lower left corner is the open after cabin devastated when its top was carried away in the storm. Photo: Author

Early spring snow quickly melts on the deck in this view looking aft. Bent turnbuckles of the port main rigging hang inboard over the bulwark at right. Photo: Author

The sliding doors were washed off the forward house by the heavy seas, exposing the interior. At right is the engine room with the winch visible. The opening at left led to the galley. Photo: Author

Fittings, line, and the spanker gaff litter the forward portion of the after cabin, bared when its top was swept away. Photo: Author

A taffrail stanchion, mast hoop, and fragments of line and sails rest on the deck of the after cabin formerly occupied by the schooner's lost master, Captain Charles Nicklas. Photo: Author

The starboard side of the after cabin remained intact. The grease line on the white paint indicates the height of the water and angle of list of the schooner when she was abandoned. Photo: Author

The steering wheel was straightened to some degree and lashed with line for the tow up Chesapeake Bay to Baltimore. Photo: Author

On the fo'c'slehead can be seen the broken club of the forestaysail and capstan. At the end of the bowsprit jutting at right is the lower portion of the metal band which held the jibboom in position. Photo: Author

The 26-inch diameter foremast was splintered at the top of the forward house as it went over the side when the schooner capsized. Photo: Author

Looking aft from the bowsprit of the *White*. Compare this with the view on page 79.
Photo: Author

As the snows melted away a more realistic picture of the wrecked schooner is revealed,
April 15. Some of her lumber cargo has been discharged. Her spanker boom and gaff,
with pieces of sail attached, may be seen at lower right. Photo: Author

During the latter part, of April 1934, the hulk was moved to McGrath's wharf in Baltimore harbor for removal of the balance of her cargo. At right is a harbor scow which had been lifted onto the pier by high water during the hurricane of August 23, 1933. Photo: Author

Looking forward in the hold of the *White* after removal of her cargo. Photo: Author

News clippings describing the trials of the *Purnell T. White* from 1924 through 1934.
Author's Collection

Chapter 8

THE next word of the *Purnell T. White* was of her sale to the firm of Weaver and Hubbard, of Baltimore. It was reported that they paid but $50 for the hull, a nominal sum merely to gain ownership and take her off the hands of R. B. White. Her next move was to that area of Baltimore harbor, in the middle branch of the Patapsco River, behind Fort McHenry. This was a ships' graveyard and hulks of several schooners, tugs, and barges littered the shallow waters. But the *White* was not there to be abandoned. She was moored alongside a World War I period wooden steamer hull, also there for storage, and "No Trespassing" signs were mounted on her bulwarks.

Workmen boarded her and started to erect a cabin and raised pilothouse over the cavity of her after deckhouse. She was to be given a new lease on life in the role of a barge. Her poop deck was cut down and aft to about half of its original length. Strongbacks were made for her hatches. Then after a feverish period of activity all work on her ceased and was never resumed. Her hold filled with water and her keel rested on the river's bottom.

On September 18, 1937, the steamer alongside her caught fire and before the flames were subdued the forward section of the *White* had been scorched. Shortly after that the new cabin structure over her after quarters was dismantled, exposing once again the splintered remains of the starboard side of her original cabin. From then on the hulk was considered abandoned.

The Baltimore and Ohio Railroad owned the property fronting the "graveyard" and used the area to dump refuse from their stations, boxcars, and other sources. When the *White* was first placed in that location she was situated a good distance offshore. But through the continuous dumping the landfill reached out, covered a number of hulks, and started cascading down on the stern of the former schooner. By 1946, her poop had been covered.

A year later the fill had inched forward to her mizzen chain plates. Trash of all description, including heavy railroad ties, covered half of the schooner to a depth of ten feet above her deck. But still the deck supported the burden. Fill had also plunged through her open after hatch and started to fill her hold. The weight had caused the vessel to settle in the river bottom mud, however, and at high tides her deck was even with the harbor's surface. During the interim she had been pillaged. Her iron capstan was removed, probably for its scrap value. But the *White* continued to point her bowsprit to the sky proudly as though defiant in her refusal to die.

After the *White* was sold, she was moored alongside a World War I wooden steamer in the ships' graveyard in the middle branch of the Patapsco River, behind Fort McHenry, Baltimore, and workmen started to convert her into a barge. A new cabin and pilothouse were erected over her shattered after cabin. In this view of May 9, 1936, her old spanker boom lies on the main deck among remnants of her rigging and fittings.
Photo: Author

Looking forward on deck as work progresses on the schooner's hull. New strongbacks for her hatches appear in the right foreground. Photo: Author

From the deck of the hulk of the two-masted schooner *Sandy Hook*, the stern of the *Purnell T. White* and her new after cabin structure may be seen, May 9, 1936.

Photo: Author

Twelve years after her dismasting at sea the *Purnell T. White* presented this appearance. Earth fill and debris had encroached upon her and were covering her stern. Even at this time, August 7, 1946, her hull was still strong and revealed little decay. The metal hull at left is of the barge *Conemaugh,* former iron full-rigged ship *Lornty,* placed there about 1940. Photo: Author

By June 2, 1947, the trash fill had reached her main hatch and high tides covered her deck. In the background are the Port Covington grain elevators. Photo: Author

There seemed to be no end to the supply of fill. Acres had been added to the shoreline and by 1948 the refuse had reached her main chain plates. Her main deck could no longer support the burden and it collapsed into the hold. The forward hatch coaming angled downward. By that time the encroachment of the fill came to a halt, at least in the direction of the *White*. A good crop of weeds and brush sprouted from the fill atop the hulk and she presented a strange picture with her bow emerging from under the embankment.

During the World War II years the oil barge *Conemaugh,* formerly the iron full-rigged ship *Lornty,* built at Liverpool in 1879, was placed along the port side of the *White*. There she stayed until 1951 when the Baltimore salvager Richard Stasch saw the scrap possibilities in this 254-foot vessel and

Debris has covered half the length of the *White* and a portion of the barge *Conemaugh* to her port. Looking aft from the fo'c'slehead in this June 2, 1947 view, can be seen the original shoreline in the far background. Photo: Author

secured title to her. During her stay in the graveyard some of the dirt fill covered her port deck and shrubs took root. After Stasch repaired the leaks in the *Conemaugh* and moved her away, the entire side of the *Purnell T. White* was exposed revealing the unbelievable depth of fill and apparent weight which covered three-quarters of her length. For the first time one could detect that, understandably, her once pronounced sheer had dropped; and there was good reason for it under that burden.

Mounted under the *White*'s fo'c'slehead was the huge metal windlass. Pillagers learned of its existence and in order to reach it so that it could be broken up and removed for its scrap value, the entire forward section of the hulk was burned back to the front of the fore cabin.

Weed-covered fill has crept up to the forward hatch of the *White* by September 9, 1948. The house shows scorching from the fire which burned a wooden steamer alongside in 1937. Photo: Author

On September 21, 1951, the barge *Conemaugh* was moved from its berth next to the *White*. Now the entire length of the former schooner is visible, showing the depth of the fill on her decks. Photo: Author

By 1957 the fill had settled into the hold of the *White* and eroded until the port side was bared once more. The hull had been forced down over the rudder post which became one of the more prominent parts of the vessel. The fragment of one lone stanchion of her taffrail stood stark on her port quarter. This seemed to hold out as evidence that the *White* had the shapeliest and most classic design of a wooden stanchion this author ever saw on a coasting schooner. I pulled it off its rod support for a keepsake. The forward deckhouse had long collapsed and its top extended over the fore hatch.

The Baltimore and Ohio had plans to build a fruit terminal on their filled area and now a decade of dumping over the *Purnell T. White* had to be undone. The huge hulk presented the problem of the erection of a heavy

The fore hatch and surrounding deck have collapsed due to the weight of the fill. The forward house is being stripped of its cypress tongue-and-groove siding, September 21, 1951. Photo: Author

pier atop this somewhat doubtful foundation. The only solution was to remove the fill which covered the *White* and then remove the hulk.

In late April 1957, workmen and equipment descended on the graveyard. A huge clamshell bucket dredge ate its way to the port side of the *White* and started to clear the fill off her deck. This chomped through her innards and brought up the tons of debris until just a water-filled shell of a ship, consisting of bottom and sides, remained. The water along both sides of the hulk was also deepened. Following the excavation work, steel beams were laid across her bulwarks and a battery of gasoline-propelled pumping units was mounted thereon. An all-out pumping effort was made to test for underwater hull leaks. It was found possible to lower the water inside her considerably before the leaks overcame the water dispersal value of the available pumps. And no turbulence was evident to indicate a severe leak.

106

Looking aft from the burned-out forepeak revealing the charred timbers, knees, and metal fastenings. Photo: Author

By April 1957, the fill on top of the *Purnell T. White* had eroded and exposed her stern. The hull had settled over the rudder post and the planking was falling off. Photo: Author

Looking forward on the burdened hulk. Her sheer is irregular and the rudder post rears its head above the deck line. Photo: Author

Mounds of earth and debris cover the sagging remnants of the former schooner but her port bulwark still appears to be strong in April 1957. Photo: Author

The forward section of the hulk was set afire so that her windlass could be salvaged for scrap. The outline of her forward house can be seen on the deck and the top of the house has collapsed onto the forward hatch coaming. Photo: Author

Looking forward over the fill toward the bow of the hulk. Photo: Author

A view from the top of the collapsed forward house, over the cutaway starboard bulwark, showing the other hulks and debris in the ships' graveyard, April 1957. Photo: Author

A clamshell bucket clears out the fill from the hull of the *White* on May 2, 1957, to make way for the construction of a fruit terminal. Photo: **Guill Photo**

Free of her solid burden, the hulk must now be pumped so that she can become water-borne and towed away, May 1957. Photo: A. Aubrey Bodine

A diver was employed to caulk her open seams with waste in conjunction with resumed pumping operations. Barehanded, he was able to detect the suction at places where this sealing was required. In a single working day he had completed the outside caulking necessary to float the hulk. One or two pumps were now able to disperse the accumulated seepage.

With the fill piled in the background, the *White* rises in the water. Photo: Author's Collection

Afloat but with water still being pumped from her hold, the *White* is moved down the middle branch of the Patapsco River by a tug to a new site of abandonment. Photo: Author's Collection

The last time the schooner was caulked was in 1933. And now, 24 years later, after the harshest treatment imaginable, and bearing a most degrading and unseaworthy appearance, the *White* became buoyant. A tug maneuvered alongside the scarred and beaten hulk and slowly eased her away from the graveyard. Water was flowing under her keel once again as her jagged bow was pointed down the Patapsco River. Her destination was a new grave site between the burned out piers of the U. S. Army near the Quarantine Station and Hawkins Point. The salvager Richard Stasch had several hulks of ships at that location and had arranged to dispose of the remains of the *White* by burning it to retrieve the metal fastenings. However, it was reported that the tug failed to place the hulk far enough inshore to expose her timbers. As a result her demolition by fire was never accomplished and she lay nestled between hulks that had been gutted by fire earlier.

Since that time I had viewed the *Purnell T. White* from the shore on several occasions, but I was determined to board her again. On May 9, 1970, I made one more visit to the old ship. Through the kindness of Buck Smith and his nephew Ross, of A. Smith and Sons Shipyard, Curtis Bay, I borrowed a 7-foot plastic dinghy to row out to the hulk from the site of the Eastalco Aluminum Company at Hawkins Point. This permitted the shortest rowing distance to the former schooner. It had been 13 years since I last boarded her, when she was still buried at the ships' graveyard near Fort McHenry.

A modern ore carrier looms in the background over the remains of the starboard bulwark and waterways on the hulk of the *Purnell T. White* as she lay abandoned off Hawkins Point, Baltimore harbor, in May 1970. Photo: Author

Transporting the dinghy to the aluminum plant in a van and setting the little craft afloat, I loaded it with tools and camera equipment. I was determined to get some pieces of her timbers and metal fittings and take a few last pictures to cover a span of 40 years I have intermittently photographed this vessel.

The hulk is situated about 500 feet off the land, her bow pointing inshore. As I approached her remnants I saw that her stern section had disappeared completely. But still standing upright and in relatively good condition, considering her 36 years of total abandonment, were a good portion of her starboard bulwark and a lesser piece of her port bulwark. Fragments of her waterways clung to the bulwarks. Her decks had vanished years ago. Several eyebolts, to which blocks and pendants were attached during her sailing days, still remained secure in the wood. A fragment of her stem broke just above water and a couple of her bobstay chain plates clung to this. Few of her hull planks remained above water. Rusting chain plates, twisted when her masts carried away in 1934, were still held in place by fittings which refused to give way.

A dusting of alumina powder from the nearby pier covered much of her timbers. Weeds were growing in the seams of her existing deck planks. Most of the hull planks seemed fairly solid. I came prepared to take a piece of these with me and selected a section between frames, clear of metal spikes, at her port bow. This measured 4 inches by 8 inches and as I put the saw to it I could feel the blade biting into solid wood. It remained thus all the way through. After I removed the foot-long piece and examined the cut, I was amazed at the excellent condition of its interior. It was yellow pine and a resinous odor could still be detected. I counted approximately 100 annual growth rings on this portion and, considering the fact that the wood has been part of the *White* for 53 years, this was a rather ancient timber.

The entire hulk of the *White* as it appeared on May 9, 1970. At extreme center left is a portion of the stem. In the foreground is the port hull planking from which the author cut a solid piece of yellow pine. In center background is the starboard bulwark with sagging waterways and deck. Photo: Author

Many of her treenails and plugs could be pulled out by hand; most of her metal fastenings resisted movement.

As I stepped off the hulk into the dinghy to return to shore I felt a certain sadness as I thought back over the 40-year period I have visited the schooner. Oh, she was a stout ship when I first knew her. Now she has deteriorated almost beyond recognition, except to me and one or two others.

These remnants of the *Purnell T. White* could last another ten or fifteen years unless the underwater portions give way—or unless progress sweeps down on the area and the hulks are cleaned out to make way for new piers.

In the meantime, her timbers look down the Patapsco River toward the Chesapeake, a route she plied many times.

Looking aft along the starboard rail and waterways of the *White* hulk, May 9, 1970.
Compare this with the same rail in the illustration on page 56. Photo: Author

Appendix

CHARLES C PAUL   R. B. WHITE   ALBERT F. PAUL

C. C. PAUL & CO.,
SHIP BROKERS AND COMMISSION MERCHANTS

C. & P. TELEPHONE
ST. PAUL 3492 & 3493

FREIGHTS PROCURED FOR
VESSELS AND BARGES

N. W. COR. FREDERICK AND PRATT STS.

VESSELS
BOUGHT AND SOLD

ENTRANCE
FREDERICK ST., 2ND FLOOR

INSURANCE EFFECTED
OYSTER SHELLS FOR SALE

BALTIMORE, MD.   February 19, 1917

The Sharptown Marine Railway Co.,
Sharptown, Md.

Dear Purnell & Connolly:

I am sending you today the blue print, specifications and contract for the machinery to go in the new vessel's forward house. Now, this is just what we have bought for the Milford vessel after going through everything with everybody in details and we find this is the cheapest and best outfit that can be gotten. We will get 5% off by taking the two outfits, otherwise we would have to pay the $1717.75 in full for each vessel.

You will notice this contract is drawn between myself and the Mianus Motor Works, Rub out R. B. White of C. C. Paul & Co., and put in there the Sharptown Marine Railway Co. Attend to this matter at once and send one copy of the contract back to the Mianus Motor Works, 321 West 42nd Street, New York.

Now, I have covered the vessel on turnbuckles. Mr. Merryman, of Whiting & Co., told us he had covered us and would guarantee the best price that could be had. I wish Connolly would get things straight and come to town for a couple of days and then we could complete everything in detail. Now, I have still heard nothing from you about the masts. Beacham can give us a price and will give us it in a day or two. We have not done anything yet about the blocks. Tell Connolly I say to get a list of these things and get his work straight so the men can keep on working and come up here, so we can straighten this matter up between us and to wire me what time to meet him at Union Station, as he can not come by steamer for a week to come.

The Schr. "IDA O. ROBINSON" is in the same position. I hope the ice will break up so it will not shove her ashore and wreck her.

Very truly yours,

RBW/WCR

R B White
WCR

117

GENERAL DIMENSIONS OF FOUR-MASTED SCHOONER
PURNELL T. WHITE

Built at Sharptown, Maryland and Completed in October 1917

Length of Keel - 165'   Length over-all on deck - 197'
Beam - 37' 9-1/2"   Depth - 14', shoalest place

Gross Tonnage - 751   Net Tonnage - 688

KEEL
Oak and Gum, 14 × 14", four lengths, two of each, with 6' scarfs bolted with eight 7/8" galvanized bolts with rings on either end. Shoeing 8 × 14", with felt between shoeing and keel, bolted to keel with 1" galvanized iron and scarfed 4' long.

FRAME
White Oak Flitch, sided 8" and doubled. Floors 8 × 14" doubled and frames diminished at plank shear to 7 × 8". The upper futtock forms the bottom stanchion. All futtocks are of the longest possible lengths to 16', and all are well bolted together with 7/8" galvanized iron, having four bolts in each futtock, spaced 24" centers, and having 1-1/4 bolt down through keel.

STEM and APRON
Stem 13 × 18" White Oak with 9" forefoot. Apron 15 × 15" through bolted into stem with bolts driven both ways 16" apart of 1-1/4" galvanized iron, well bolted to deadwood and keel.

STERN POST
White Oak, 17 × 18" with tenons into keel, well bolted with 1-1/4" galvanized iron into keel and deadwood.

TRANSOM
White Oak, 16 × 18" well bolted into stern-post with 1-1/8" galvanized iron, which forms deck beam. Main deck all fastened to transom.

PLANKING
Square fastened with two 7/8" galvanized headed bolts and two 1-1/4" locust treenails, also edge bolted with 1" galvanized bolts. Planking from garboard up to covering board 4" thick and fastened with two spikes 7-16 × 8" and two 1-1/4" treenails.

CEILING
Yellow Pine. Dead flat 4" thick, about six streaks. From dead flat to plank shear 8" thick running continuously from stem to after transom or arch board. All ceiling scarfed with 4' scarfs and fastened with two galvanized 7/8" bolts and edge bolted between every other frame. In addition to the galvanized iron fastening about 90 per cent of the treenails driven from the outside come through and are wedged. The 8" ceiling picks up the outer end of the Short Floor Timbers.

KEELSONS
Main keelson, three in number, yellow pine, 14 × 14" with keyed scarfs 6' long, running from stem to stern-post and forming part of dead wood, fastened with two 1-1/4" galvanized bolts in each frame down through keel.

1ST RIDER
Yellow pine, 14 × 14", scarfs and lengths same as main keelson, fastened with two 1-1/4" galvanized bolts through keel, and edge bolted every other frame.

2ND RIDER
Yellow pine, scarfs and lengths same as 1st rider, bolted every 8" with 1-1/8" galvanized bolts 39" long, driven through clinch rings. Sister Keelsons, four streaks, scarfed and fastened as main keelson and driven through rings.

118

DEADWOODS

Yellow pine sided 14" and well fastened with 1-1/4" galvanized iron bolts, driven through two and into the third streak.

DECK FRAMES

All hatch beams and Poop Deck beams, yellow pine, 12 × 14", gained into clamps, crowned 6", worked 2" and sprung 4". All other beams 12 × 12" and spaced 30" between, fastened in clamps with two 1" galvanized bolts. Hatch Carlins, yellow pine, 10 × 10" fastened in the same manner.

KNEES

Hackmatack, one under each beam and under all carlins. Knees sided 8" under main beams and 7" under carlins, and are all fastened with 7/8" galvanized iron driven through rings.

STANCHIONS

Oak, 8 × 14" and 8 × 12", one under each beam, bolted with 7/8" galvanized iron at bottom and fastened at top with 3/8 × 4" iron strapped over beam, two bolts in each end.

POINTERS

Two sets forward and two sets aft, 10 × 12", well bolted, with hooks on each set, bolts 1-1/8" iron driven through rings.

WATERWAYS

Yellow pine, one streak on top of beam 12 × 12", scarfed 6' and bolted down through beams with 7/8" headed bolts and bolted through bends and frame with 7/8" headed bolts driven from outside. Two 10 × 12" yellow pine lock streaks, dovetailed down over beams 2", having 6' scarfs and in long lengths which continues from stem to after transom, bolted down through beams with 7/8" headed bolts, also edge bolted through frame at each intersection. Covering Board 5 × 16" in long lengths, bolted down through three streaks of bends and wedged around top timbers with white pine edges and edge bolted through top timbers.

DECKING

Main decking 4 × 4" in long lengths, fastened to and extending over main transom to after transom, fastened with 7 16 × 8" galvanized spikes and plugged with white pine plugs. House tops, Quarter and Forecastle deck all fastened the same and of same dimensions. Four streaks 6 × 12" in center extending from apron to poop deck forming a very substantial partner. These are fastened with 5/8 × 12" galvanized spikes and plugged with white pine plugs.

RAIL STRINGERS

Are 6 × 10" in long lengths and scarfed, also gained in on top timbers 2" making a solid bed for rail to rest on, fastened to these with 7/8" galvanized headed bolts driven from outside and clinched on rings inside, two at each intersection.

MAIN RAIL

Yellow pine, 6 × 15", long lengths, and 6' lock scarfs, having six treenails in each scarf well bolted down into stringers and top stanchions with 7/8" galvanized headed bolts 18" apart and 15" long, being 3'4" above covering board.

WAIST

Yellow Pine 3" thick, fastened with 5" galvanized spikes, plugged with white pine plugs. Five streaks in long lengths.

POOP DECK

Is covered with 8 × 12" yellow pine which forms stringers for deck frame and is fastened with 1/2 × 10" galvanized spikes and is edge bolted. Poop deck beams, yellow pine, 8 × 12" and 6 × 12". Lazarette Hatch at forward end of house, also one aft alongside of wheel box. Bitts, two sets 12 × 12", yoked with 4" flitch and edge fastened with treenails.

HATCHES

Are 12'6" × 12'6" inside measurement, and three in number, coamings 24" above the deck. Hatch covering divided into eight small hatches, each covered with native cypress and caulked. Well protected with galvanized iron.

POOP DECK BULKHEAD

One piece 8 × 12" on Main Deck, one 5 × 10", one 8 × 10", one 6 × 11", one 4 × 8", one 6 × 10", all yellow pine, bolted with 1" iron 18" apart and four through bolts all the way through beam, 1-1/8" with nut on lower end and set up.

SALTING

Well salted down as far as air streaks will permit amidship, and forward and after cants are packed in deadwood. All spaces under Poop Deck are packed to covering board or deck frame.

LAZARETTE

Forward and aft of cabin with 3' square hatch, with coaming raised about 15" above deck. Is also very roomy with alley on each side of cabin with port side partitioned off for cook's provisions, also shelves for storage opening into pantry.

CAULKING

Garboard streaks, two threads cotton and five threads oakum hawsed well back and payed with pitch. From covering board to garboard, two threads of cotton hawsed back and three threads of oakum well hawsed back and payed with pitch to light water and with white seam paint above water line, three coats.

PAINTING

Outside, one priming coat and two finishing coats all above light water, and two coats of copper paint below light water. Cabin finished in natural wood, sufficient coats to make a good job.

SAILS

Full suit of sails and covers. Lower sails of No. 0 canvas and lighter ones of suitable number.

WATER TANKS

One iron water tank in hold forward of about 1500 gallons capacity, and the one in the hold aft of about 1000 gallons capacity.

WINDLASS

No. 8, of Knowlton make for 1-3/4" chain attached to power equipment with messenger chain. One set of patent riders of Hyde make, installed in proper position.

ENGINE

One 12 to 16 H.P. Mianus equipment complete with cargo hoist, winch heads, power pumps and all shafting and sprocket chains for connecting same in usual manner for a four-mast schooner.

SPARS

Foremast 89' × 26", Mainmast 89'6" × 25", Mizzen 90'6" × 24", Spanker 91'6" × 24", Spanker Boom 60' × 16", Jib-boom 56' × 16", Fore-Topmast 51' × 16", Bow Sprit 45' long, 26" square. All the above are of Oregon Pine. All other spars made of northern spruce in proportionate sizes.

RIGGING

Of Roeblings best wire. All standing rigging of 3-1/2 wire, remainder of wire rigging equipment is amply large in proportion, all spliced into turnbuckles, and served up and down 10'. Bobstays 1-1/4" galvanized chain. All outboard rigging of galvanized chain.

HALYARD AND RUNNING RIGGING

Halyards of Manila 3-1/4". Sheets 3-1/2", rigged complete with one coil 5-1/2" and one towing hawser 7-1/2".

BLOCKS

One set of 14" blocks made by Western Block Co.

RUDDER BRACES

Three set composition.

ANCHORS AND CHAINS

180 fathoms of 1-3/4" Stud Link Chain, tested. Two 3500 lb. stockless Bowers, tested, and one 500 lb. Kedge.

YAWL

One 22 ft. Yawl 7-1/2 H.P., Mianus motor installed complete.

FORWARD HOUSE

Frame of Yellow Pine, sheathed diagonally with tongued and grooved first pine and then sheathed over horizontally with 7/8" tongued and grooved No. 1 Gulf Cypress.

CABIN

Framed of Yellow Pine from Main Deck and sheathed in same manner as forward house. Cabin of Coach House pattern, with skylight in after cabin, also raised companionway aft. Cabin is 29'8" long and 24' wide, all of No. 1 grade material and workmanship.

PORTS

Two Bow Ports, one in each bow 30" × 30".

CLASSIFICATION

American Bureau of Shipping, classed A1 for 15 years.

The above is a full and complete description of the four-masted schooner just completed at the yards of the Sharptown Marine Railway Co., Sharptown, Maryland. All Georgia Pine is of selected prime grade, 1905 rules. The frame is all of the best quality native White Oak, and the workmanship throughout is of the highest class.

ALONZO R. CONLEY
Designer and Builder

SPECIFICATION SHEET---

for one new vessel.

New York, February 10, 1917.

Mr. R. B. White,
c/o C. C. Paul & Co.
Cor. Frederick & Pratt Sts.,
Baltimore, Md.

One...16HP. Mianus four cycle two cylinder gasoline engine, vertical type, mounted on a back-geared base, gear ratio 2 to 1, engine speed 400 r.p.m.
weight, 3000 lbs. one small fuel tank, battery outfit, pipe and fittings and
water tank.
Price complete............................. $725.00
Dimensions and measurements as per attached blue-print.

One... Winch Hoist "L" (page 11, of Mianus catalogue of gasoline outfits for vessels), consisting of
1 - main shaft, coupled in two pieces, 2-15/16 × 25 ft. long
2 - Winch Heads 8 × 12; 2-pawls and brackets
5 - Axle Boxes; 2-Collars
1 - Sprocket wheel 10t × 88
1 - Sprocket wheel 36t × 88
20 ft. sprocket chain 88, 1 - chain coupler 88
10 - Machine bolts and washers 3/4 × 12
Price complete............................. $167.50

One... Cargo Friction Drum hoist, dimensions of drum 12 × 24; capacity 2000
pounds on a single line (see page 18). Sprocket drive for hoist as follows:
1 - Sprocket wheel 18t × 103
1 - Sprocket wheel 12t × 103
1 - Jaw Clutch (Main shaft); 2-keys 5/8
No sprocket chain.
Price complete............................. $228.25

One... Centrifugal Pump (Goulds) No. 5; 6" suction 5" discharge, fitted with
bronze impeller and bronze shaft, foot valve and strainer. The top of this
pump to be connected to deck pump with 3/4" pipe with fittings and valves
so that the deck pump can be used to prime the Centrifugal pump. Sprocket
drive for pump as follows:
1 - sprocket wheel 15t × 103
1 - sprocket wheel 12t × 103
20 ft. of chain 103; 1-chain coupler 103
2 - keys 5/8
Price complete without suction or discharge pipe.. $250.00

One... Mianus Hooded Pump with pump attachment
"M" (no pipe included)................................... $ 60.00

One... Excelsior deck pump No. 8 horizontal 1-1/2" suction × 1-1/4" discharge
fitted with eccentric drive so that it can be connected to the main shaft, set
up and attached to main shaft (no pipe included).............. $ 60.00

One... Windlass Attachment special consisting of
    1 - counter shaft 2-7/16 × 4' long
    2 - axle boxes
    1 - sprocket 28t × 103
    1 - clutch sprocket 8t × 103
    1 - Clamp clutch instead of Jaw clutch
 40 ft. sprocket chain 103
    1 - chain coupler
    2 - keys 5/8
    2 - collars
    4 - bolts and washers 3/4 × 12
            Price complete............................... $ 67.00

Installing at Sharptown, Maryland, freight and cartage........ $160.00
                                                     $1717.75

MIANUS MOTOR WORKS

MEMORANDUM OF SAILS

Memorandum of sails - schooner Purnell T. White

September 21, 1922		Maker of sails
New topsail, 148 yards #5 canvas	$100.64	Stevenson-Magee
New spanker	$389.00	Stevenson-Magee

....

January 9, 1924		
Flying jib, #1 Woodberry duck	$160.00	Lewis Martin & Son

....

September 1923		
Mizzensail	$300.00	Portland Sailmaking Co.

....

April 12, 1924		
Fore, main, and mizzen topsails #4 duck	$350.00	Taulane
Forestaysail 2/0 duck	$125.00	"
Foresail 2/0 duck	$300.00	"

....

November 11, 1925		
Mainsail #0 cotton duck 409 yards	$399.53	Lewis Martin & Son

....

June 3, 1924		
Spanker (made for schooner Charles D. Stanford)	$465.00	Taulane

....

July 19, 1926

3 brown waterproof tarpaulins	$ 90.00	Taulane

. . . .

August 31, 1926

Mainsail	$325.00	Taulane

. . . .

November 3, 1926

Foresail	$310.00	Taulane
Forestaysail	$130.00	"
Jib	$120.00	"
Flying jib	$110.00	"

. . . .

November 16, 1926

Spanker	$450.00	Taulane

. . . .

November 25, 1927

Foretopsail #4 duck	$110.00	Taulane
Maintopsail #4 duck	$110.00	"

. . . .

March 14, 1928

Spanker topsail #4 duck	$115.00	Taulane

. . . .

September 5, 1929

Maintopsail #4 duck	$110.00	Taulane

. . . .

September 9, 1930

Mainsail #0 duck	$320.00	Taulane

. . . .

September 19, 1930

Spanker #1/0	$445.00	Marshall & Godfrey

. . . .

November 6, 1930

3 hatch covers #4 waterproof duck	$ 92.50	Marshall & Godfrey

. . . .

January 12, 1931

Forestaysail #0 duck	$125.00	Taulane

. . . .

December 1, 1932

Mizzensail #1/0 duck	$231.00	Marshall & Godfrey

. . . .

CONTRACT

Contract made and concluded this 10th day of February, 1917, by and between the Mianus Motor Works, of Stamford, Connecticut, New York Office, #321 West 42nd Street, New York City, party of the first part, The Sharptown Marine Railway Company, Sharptown, Md., party of the second part.

WITNESSETH: That the party of the first part agrees to and with the second part to furnish and install on a new schooner which they are now building at Sharptown, Maryland, the following articles of machinery and fittings, as per attached specification sheet dated February 10, 1917.

1 - 16HP. Mianus Back-geared four cycle engine
1 - Winch Hoist "L"
1 - Cargo Hoist 10 × 24 with sprocket drive
1 - Centrifugal Pump (Goulds) 6" suction   5" discharge
1 - Mianus Hooded Pump and Pump Attachment "M"
1 - Excelsior Deck Pump and Attachment
1 - Windlass Attachment for Hyde Windlass

DELIVERY: The first part agrees to deliver the above machinery and fittings alongside of vessel at Sharptown, Maryland, on or before June 1st, 1917 and to pay all charges for freight and cartage. The second part agrees to place this machinery on board of vessel.

INSTALLING: The first part agrees to furnish a competent man to set up and install the above machinery in good working order. Installing to consist of placing engine, fuel tank, water tank, battery outfit, Winch Hoist "L", Centrifugal Pump, Cargo Hoist, Mianus Hooded Pump and Pump Attachment "M", Excelsior Deck Pump and Attachment, Windlass Attachment for Hyde Windlass in position as shown on drawing No. 8295 attached and to fasten the same to the woodwork of vessel and to make all the necessary connections.

CARPENTER WORK: The second part agrees to have the deck house built and ready for this machinery at the time the installing is required. The second part also agrees to furnish all lumber and carpenter work for the building of foundation for engine, Pump and Cargo Hoist and to set up a foundation for fuel tank to make a rack or battery case, bore all necessary holes for bolts in the woodwork and any other necessary carpenter work that may be required. The second part agrees to do this carpenter work promptly when called upon to do so by the first part or their representative.

PAYMENT: The second part agrees to pay to the first part promptly on completion of this contract, the sum of One Thousand Seven Hundred Seventeen Dollars, and seventy-five cents ($1717.75), lawful money of the United States, less 5% discount.

For the true and faithful performance of this contract the parties hereunto bind themselves each in the penal of sum of One Dollar ($1.00) for failure to do so as agreed.

SIGNED, SEALED AND DELIVERED

in the presence of

THE MIANUS MOTOR WORKS

Chas A Allyn L.S.

Treas

Hampton Mackle L.S.

P White *Sec*

—————————

E H Cooper

OWNERS OF THE PURNELL T. WHITE

First Certificate of Enrollment   October 22, 1917

White Shipping Company, Albert W. Robinson, President, was sole owner of this schooner. The certificate was surrendered at Crisfield, Maryland, December 18, 1917, as the property changed. The new owners then appeared as: R.B. White, Salisbury, Maryland, 50/161; Albert W. Robinson, Laurel, Delaware, 50/161; George W. Woolford, Cambridge, Maryland, 17/161; A. R. Conley, 17/161; P.T. White, 17/161; B.P. Gravenor, 10/161 - all of Sharptown, Maryland.

Ownership remained the same until the enrollment of March 21, 1922. At that time Mary A. Gravenor took over from B.P. Gravenor.

Next change in ownership occurred on enrollment of June 2, 1923. R.B. White, managing owner, 32/161; A.W. Robinson, 50/161; George W. Woolford 17/161; A.R. Conley, 17/161; P.T. White, 17/161; Mary A. Gravenor, 10/161; Lewis B. Taulane, 2/161; Edward G. Taulane, 2/161, Philadelphia; Wm. H. Swan, New York, 4/161; Redman-Vane Shipbuilding Co., Baltimore, 4/161; C.C. Paul & Co., Baltimore, 6/161.

The enrollment of December 9, 1926 indicated that Mary A. Gravenor dropped out and R.B. White increased his ownership to 42/161. Others remained the same.

A new enrollment as a result of property partly changed indicated that Albert W. Robinson dropped out and R.B. White increased his ownership to 92/161. Others remained the same.

Enrollment surrendered April 18, 1935 - Ship abandoned.

NORFOLK. ....April 1, 1927.... 19...

RECEIVED FROM WILLIAM H. SWAN & SONS, INC.
4 COMMERCE STREET

FOR   Schr. Purnell T. White

DESTINATION   Newport News

Stores

1	bbl.	Flour
1	"	Family Beef
1	"	Clear Pork
1	Keg	Pigs Feet
1	doz.	can Tripe
6	lbs.	Hams Wrapped
	"	Bacon "
75	"	Lard in tins
30	"	Cabin Butter
30	"	Crew Butter
12	"	Y. A. Cheese
2	5 lb. pkg.	Graham Flour
12	pkg.	Corn Meal
10	lbs.	Rye Meal
5	pkg.	Hominy Grits
12	"	Pancake Flour
6	"	Ro. Oats
6	"	Cream Wheat
1	box	Pilot Bread 24 lbs.
20	lbs.	Cabin Rice
10	"	Split Peas
10	"	Green Peas
50	"	White Beans
15	"	R. K. Beans
20	"	Lima Beans
6	pkg.	Tapioca
6	"	Sage
4	"	Barley
12	"	Macaroni
3	"	Vermecelli
6	"	Corn Starch
29	lbs.	N. F. Cod
3	Kits	Mackerel
1	"	Tongues & Sounds
18	pkg.	Table Salt
4	Bags	Potatoes (600 lbs.)
100	lbs.	Onions
1	doz.	can Beets
4	lbs.	Cabin Tea
40	"	Cabin Coffee grd. in tins
6	"	Cocoa
100	"	Sugar
2	gal.	Mollasses
2	"	Karo Syrup
2	"	Vinegar
8	lbs.	Raisins
4	"	Currants
15	"	Prunes
15	"	Evap. Apples
1	"	Grd. Nutmeg
½	"	" Mace
1	"	" Cinnamon
1	"	" Allspice
2	"	Blk. Pepper
1	"	Cream Tartar
24	pkg.	Magic Yeast
6	tins	Royal Baking Powder
1	pkg.	Sage

6	bot.	Chow Chow	
12	"	Mixed Pickles	
2	"	Worcestershire	
3	"	Table Oil	
½	doz.	can Peaches	
½	"	" Pears	
½	"	" Pineapple	
½	"	" Plums	
2	"	" Salmon	
1	"	" Sardines	
2	doz.	can Kipp. Herring	
16	"	" Evap. Milk	Small size
4	"	" Cond. Milk	
2	"	" Roast Beef	
1	"	" Mutton	
1	"	" Vienna Sausage	
1	"	" Clams	
2	"	" Peas	
2	"	" Str. Beans	
2	"	" Tomatoes	
½	"	" Mince Meat	
1	"	" Corn Beef	
1	"	jars Cabin Jam	
2	lbs.	Baking Soda	
2	doz.	can Asstd. Soups	
6	lbs.	Shr. Coccanut	
2	pkg.	Summer Savory	
30	doz.	Eggs	
6	bot.	Tomato Catsup	
1	bu.	Apples	
1	doz.	can Sauerkraut	

Chas Nickolas
Master —

RECEIVED FROM WILLIAM H. SWAN & SONS, INC.
4 COMMERCE STREET

FOR   Schr. Purnell T. White

DESTINATION   Newport News

Chandlery

1	gro. Economy Matches
2	cakes Sapolic
4	doz. cakes Laundry Soap
1	set Bricks for #28 Mascot
4	Coffee Mugs
2	Agate Berlin Kettles B. H. 4 qts.
1	" " " " 10 "
1	Fruit Dish
1	Soup Tureen
100	fthm. 2-1/2" Plymouth Manila 113 lbs.
100	" 2-3/4" " " 136 "
100	" 1-3/4" " " 68 "
16	lbs. 2 Y. Manila Spunyarn
10	ft. 3-1/2" Hemp Lanyard
10	ft. 3" " "
4	Sewing Palms
1	doz. #12 Sail Needles
1	" #13 " "
10	Balls Sail Twine
32	yds. 10oz. Duck
2	#4 Sash Tools
2	#6 " "
2	2" Flat Paint Brushes
8	28" Mast Hoops
200	gal. Gasoline Direct by Phillips & Co.
1	Metal Drum Kerosene 57 gal.
75	lbs. White Lead
75	" " Zinc
10	gal. Raw Oil
1	" Interior Varnish
1	" White Shellac
2	" I.S. White Paint
3	" Green Paint
10	" Deck Varnish
1	" Japan Dryer
1	" Vermillion Red Paint
1	" Smoke Stack Black
1	qt. Aluminum
1	gal. Get Em Insecticide
25	lbs. White Rags
12	cans Lye
12	pkg. Washing Powder large
1	Dust Brush
1	Dust Pan
1	#7 Corn Broom
4	#8 Deck Corn Brooms
1	doz. sheets Emery Cloth
1	" " Sandpaper
1	lb. Galv. Tacks
2	Galv. Pails
10	lbs. 3" Wire Nails
20	lbs. Sparine
1	Galv. Funnell with Strainer
1	Oil Feeder with long spout
2	qts. Metal Polish
4	B. Lip Hinge Burners
6	B. Chimnies

6	B. Lip Chimnies
3	6 cell Hot Shot Batteries
6	#6 Dry Cell Batteries
5	gal. Mobile Oil A.
1	bot. 3 & 1 Oil
4	Crew Mattresses
4	Colored Pillow Cases
4	Colored Sheets

Mail
, Trunk

Chas Nickles
Master

Any thing wrong
I let you
know from
Georgetown

Index

129

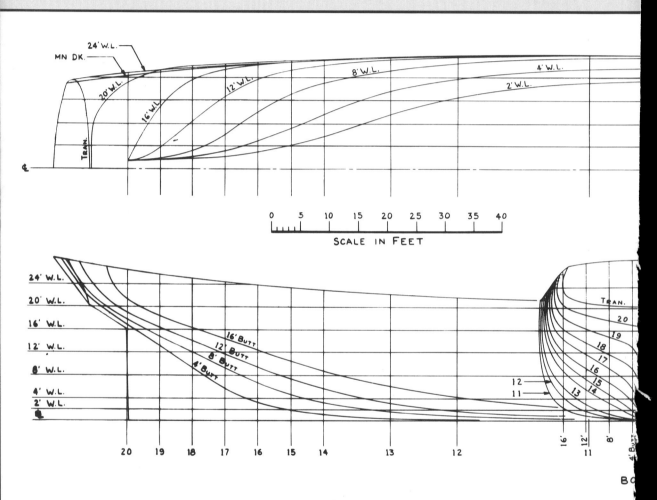

24' W.L.
MN DK.
20' W.L.
16' W.L.
12' W.L.
8' W.L.
4' W.L.
2' W.L.
TRAN.

0   5   10   15   20   25   30   35   40
SCALE IN FEET

24' W.L.
20' W.L.
16' W.L.
12' W.L.
8' W.L.
4' W.L.
2' W.L.

16' BUTT
12' BUTT
8' BUTT
4' BUTT

TRAN.
20
19
18
17
16
15
14
13
12
11

16'   12'   8'   4' BUTT

20   19   18   17   16   15   14   13   12   11

BO